# MARY MCLEOD BETHUNE

| 1920 | 1930 | 1940 | 1950 | 1960 | 1970 | 1980 | 1990 | 2000 | 2010 |
|------|------|------|------|------|------|------|------|------|------|
| 1925 | 1935 | 1945 | 1955 | 1965 | 1975 | 1985 | 1995 | 2005 | 2015 |

# CIVIL RIGHTS LEADERS

Al Sharpton

Coretta Scott King

James Farmer

Jesse Jackson

Malcolm X

Martin Luther King Jr.

Mary McLeod Bethune

Rosa Parks

Thurgood Marshall

# MARY MCLEOD BETHUNE

Mary Hasday

MASON CREST

Mason Crest
450 Parkway Drive, Suite D
Broomall, Pennsylvania 19008
(866) MCP-BOOK (toll-free)
www.masoncrest.com

Printed and bound in the United States of America.

CPSIA Compliance Information: Batch #CRL2018.
For further information, contact Mason Crest at 1-866-MCP-Book.

First printing
1 3 5 7 9 8 6 4 2

Library of Congress Cataloging-in-Publication Data on file at the Library of Congress.

ISBN: 978-1-4222-4009-0 (hc)
Civil Rights Leaders series ISBN: 978-1-4222-4002-1

Publisher's Note: Websites listed in this book were active at the time of publication. The publisher is not responsible for websites that have changed their address or discontinued operation since the date of publication. The publisher reviews and updates the websites each time the book is reprinted.

**QR CODES AND LINKS TO THIRD-PARTY CONTENT**
You may gain access to certain third-party content ("Third-Party Sites") by scanning and using the QR Codes that appear in this publication (the "QR Codes"). We do not operate or control in any respect any information, products, or services on such Third-Party Sites linked to by us via the QR Codes included in this publication, and we assume no responsibility for any materials you may access using the QR Codes. Your use of the QR Codes may be subject to terms, limitations, or restrictions set forth in the applicable terms of use or otherwise established by the owners of the Third-Party Sites. Our linking to such Third-Party Sites via the QR Codes does not imply an endorsement or sponsorship of such Third-Party Sites or the information, products, or services offered on or through the Third-Party Sites, nor does it imply an endorsement or sponsorship of this publication by the owners of such Third-Party Sites.

**PHOTO CREDITS:** Library of Congress: pg. 1, 6, 8, 16, 33, 37, 40, 45, 49, 57, 62, 64, 67, 70, 73, 76, 78, 81, 82, 87, 96, 98, 100, 104, 111, 112, 116, 119, 120; Everett Historical: pg. 11, 14, 21, 24, 38, 46, 49; Shutterstock, Inc.: pg. 18, 108; Bethune-Cookman College: pg. 24; State Archives of Florida: pg. 27; Culver Pictures: pg. 28; Government & Heritage Library, State Library of NC: pg. 30; Wikimedia Commons: pg. 41, 59; National Archives: pg. 85.

# TABLE OF CONTENTS

# KEY ICONS TO LOOK FOR:

**Words to Understand:** These words with their easy-to-understand definitions will increase the reader's understanding of the text while building vocabulary skills.

**Sidebars:** This boxed material within the main text allows readers to build knowledge, gain insights, explore possibilities, and broaden their perspectives by weaving together additional information to provide realistic and holistic perspectives.

**Educational Videos:** Readers can view videos by scanning our QR codes, providing them with additional educational content to supplement the text. Examples include news coverage, moments in history, speeches, iconic sports moments and much more!

**Text-Dependent Questions:** These questions send the reader back to the text for more careful attention to the evidence presented there.

**Research Projects:** Readers are pointed toward areas of further inquiry connected to each chapter. Suggestions are provided for projects that encourage deeper research and analysis.

**Series Glossary of Key Terms:** This back-of-the book glossary contains terminology used throughout this series. Words found here increase the reader's ability to read and comprehend higher-level books and articles in this field.

Ridgewood Avenue in Daytona Beach, Florida, circa 1920.
When Mary McLeod Bethune arrived in Daytona in 1904,
the coastal town—like most places in the South—lacked
a school where blacks could receive a formal education.
She promptly founded her own institute, and by 1920 it
had an enrollment of almost 300 students.

# WORDS TO UNDERSTAND

poll tax—a fee that people were required to pay in order to vote.
Today this is illegal in the United States.

resolute—purposeful, determined, and unwavering.

white supremacy—a belief that white people are superior to people
of all other races, especially the black race, and should therefore
dominate society.

# CHAPTER 1

# TARGET OF THE KLAN

As Mary Mcleod Bethune rode her bicycle through the resort town of Daytona Beach, Florida, late in the summer of 1920, she hardly acted like someone who had recently become the target of death threats. A hefty, **resolute** woman of 45, she cheerfully greeted the area's black residents as she pedaled from house to house, urging the local women to exercise their newly won right to vote. And they in turn greeted the founder of the community's first school for blacks, which she had established 16 years earlier.

Bethune had started the Daytona Normal and Industrial Institute for Negro Girls (which later became Bethune-Cookman College) with $1.50 in cash, five pupils, and a few packing cases that served as desks. She had raised additional money for the school by baking pies and selling ice cream to railroad construction workers. As the school began to grow, she solicited funds from leading philanthropists, industrialists, and black organizations. Her shrewd business skills and help from both the local black community and the area's wealthy white residents enabled the school to expand rapidly from a small cottage to a trim, well-kept campus housing Daytona Beach's first black hospital.

Bethune also took an interest in other educational matters, including a proposed bill on the general ballot in 1920 that provided for the first public high school for

From the time they were first given the ballot following the Civil War, eligible black voters in the South were constantly harassed and pressured by whites who sought, illegally, to "fix" elections.

blacks in Daytona Beach. This proposal was a major issue between the two candidates who were running for the office of mayor. One candidate was violently opposed to the school, whereas the other candidate promised not only to build the school but to construct better streets, lighting, and sewers in the black section of town.

Bethune canvassed the black women in Daytona Beach as the election drew near, telling them to register to vote if they had not already done so and urging them to go to the polls on election day. Their votes were crucial, she said, because the upcoming election would directly affect the education of blacks in the community.

## VOTING IN THE SOUTH

Although the U.S. Constitution granted all American citizens the right to vote, many of the nation's southern states sought to limit the participation of blacks in the electoral process. In certain areas, only blacks who owned property or who could read and write to the satisfaction of the registrar (who was usually white) were eligible to vote. In some instances, blacks had to provide character references from white sponsors before they were allowed to vote. These references were mainly given when a black voter and his sponsor favored the same candidate.

Blacks were also excluded from voting in primaries, which meant they had little say in choosing the candidates for an election. The most notorious device for preventing blacks from voting, however, was the **poll tax**, a voting fee of $1 or $2 that often put political representation beyond the reach of southern farmers, who earned as little as $100 a year. Enacted in 1885, Florida's poll tax was not repealed until 1945.

Even when blacks were able to emerge from this maze of voting restrictions, intimidation or violence was often a problem on election day. Organizations such as the Constitutional Guards and White Brotherhood in North Carolina and the Men of Justice in Alabama led to the establishment of the **white supremacist** group known as the Ku Klux Klan. Founded as a social club at Pulaski, Tennessee, in 1866, the Klan represented all that was backward, malicious, and racist. It carried out a masked, violent campaign of terror against blacks, burning crosses in black neighborhoods, making death threats—even maiming and killing in an attempt to intimidate blacks from exercising their newly won civil rights.

The Klan was so successful in its intimidation tactics that that federal laws were passed to curb its activities, and the organization disbanded by the late 1870s. But in 1915 the Klan was re-formed, although with a different goal in mind. Whereas the original organization had been formed by southern whites to improve their social status once blacks won unprecedented privileges and opportunities following the Civil War, the new Klan did not seek to change the social order. Instead, it became dedicated solely to the idea of white supremacy. Anyone who was not white, Anglo-Saxon, and born in America became its enemy.

Bethune's canvassing efforts in 1920 quickly made her a target of the Klan. Hearing of her voter registration drive and her determination to defeat the mayoral candidate whom the Klan supported, Klan members made threats on her life. Bethune continued her organizing activities despite the threats of reprisal from the Klan; she was determined never to give in to it. "Faith and courage, patience and fortitude," she counseled, "social change cannot happen quickly." She told her followers, "Use your minds, but keep your lips closed.… Don't be afraid of the Klan! Quit running! Hold your head up high. Look every man straight in the eye and make no apology to anyone because of … color. When you see a burning cross remember the son of God who bore the heaviest cross of all."

# AN ATTEMPT TO INTIMIDATE

The Klan marched to the Daytona Normal and Industrial Institute on the night before the 1920 mayoral election, but their visit did not take Bethune by surprise. They had tried to frighten her a few years earlier—also before an important election—and this time she was more than ready for them.

Bethune helped to unify black voters in Daytona Beach so that they would not be intimidated at the polls by groups like the Ku Klux Klan.

The sounds of horses galloping and horns being blown outside the school grounds signaled to Bethune, in the school's main building, that the Klan was drawing near. She went to a window to look for them and discovered that all the streetlights beyond the campus had been turned off. The Klan, which had infiltrated many churches, police departments, and municipal services in the South, had arranged to plunge the area into complete darkness to frighten Bethune and others who planned to vote.

Bethune could dimly make out a parade of about 100 robed figures walking along Second Avenue. At the head of the procession was a cross that burned menacingly large and bright. There was a strange, unearthly silence as the Klan went past the school's front gate and filed up the drive. Then one of the girls watching from a nearby fire escape started to scream, and like a chain reaction others joined in the mounting hysteria.

# THE KU KLUX KLAN

Groups of white men that slaves often called "paddyrollers" served as the outside enforcement arm for slaveholders. While denying any connection to theses provocateurs, "paddyrollers" could be dispatched to capture wayward slaves, physically intimidate both slaves and free persons of color, or exact the ultimate punishment in the form of a horrifying death.

With the demise of slavery at the end of the Civil War, the threat of a new and decidedly colorful power structure triggered some Southern land barons and businessmen to protect their wealthy status by relying on violence and intimidation similar to the "paddyrollers" of yesteryear. The Ku Klux Klan was one such organization, established in May 1866 in Pulaski, Tennessee, by members of the former Confederate Army. It originated in a period of time when the South lived under Union military rule and a start was made to give black men equal rights in law as well as practice. Blacks were a political majority in many southern states and, in some minds, required tight control.

Members of the Ku Klux Klan came together supposedly for social purposes. It were a fraternal order of white businessmen, politicians, and workers, and indeed a Klansman could be the sheriff, mayor, or banker. However, the fraternal order was dedicated to keeping blacks on the lowest rungs of the political and economic ladders. Marauding Klansmen threatened blacks who tried to leave plantations and operate their own farms. Their brutality impacted the 1866 elections and grew more organized at shutting out the newly granted black vote. The Klan and other similar white supremacist groups so terrorized black communities that a law was passed to stem their terrorism. The 1871 Force Bill helped to reduce the violence against freedmen, though it did not end completely.

Around 1915, the Ku Klux Klan experienced a resurgence, and Klan membership ranged from four to five million across the nation during the 1920s. This new Klan did not only target African Americans. They also directed their violence toward other ethnic and religious groups, such as new immigrants, Jews, and Roman Catholics. A burning cross in front of the homes of victims became the new Klan's calling card.

Most black men, women, and children living in the South during the 1920s and 1930s were taught how to avoid, or at least survive, attacks by white supremacists. Still, thousand of African Americans lost their lives. The membership and influence of the Ku Klux Klan dwindled in the 1940s, but the organization experienced a revival during the civil rights movement of the 1950s and 1960s. Members of this white supremacist group still exist in the United States, although their activities were curtailed in the 1980s by a series of lawsuits won on behalf of victims by the Southern Poverty Law Office. Today the Klan's membership is estimated at around 5,000 people nationwide.

Hidden behind their masks and long white robes, a line of Ku Klux Klan members hold a ceremony in front of a burning cross. The Klan's nighttime raids on institutions such as Bethune's school were meant to terrorize people who were trying to improve conditions for blacks.

But it would take more than men garbed in white to frighten Bethune. Although the Klan controlled the town's streetlights, it did not have power over the school's electricity. As the masked and hooded men encircled the drive, blowing horns and waving the burning cross, she ordered all the lights in the building to be shut off and those outside on the campus to be turned on. This should be done, she said, "so they'll know that *we're* home!" Frightened students ran from room to room following her instructions.

Within a matter of moments, Bethune and her staff could clearly observe the actions of the white-robed men in the glare of the campus spotlights. The Klan's tactics had been reversed. The vigilantes now had eyes watching *them* while the school's students and teachers were shrouded under a blanket of darkness.

Suddenly, a strong, loud voice rang out amid the panic. "Be not dismayed whate'er betide," sang one of Bethune's students, "God will take care of us." Soon, a chorus of voices—nervous at first, then imbued with the strength and force of numbers—echoed the sentiment.

The Klansmen, realizing that their intimidation tactics had been unsuccessful, left the campus and disappeared into the night.

Bethune went to the polls the following morning and saw two signs posted outside the election site: One sign indicated where whites were to line up to vote; the other sign indicated where black voters were to stand. The signs meant that she and the other blacks would have to wait until all of the white voters had filed in and out.

Undeterred, Bethune spent the entire day walking up and down the line of registered black voters, making it a point to talk with them and quiet their fears. They were finally called in to cast their ballots just before closing time. She later reported, "I was standing at the polling place at 8 o'clock with a line of Negros behind me. They kept us waiting all day, but WE VOTED!"

When the votes were counted, the candidate whom the Klan supported had been defeated. Bethune's unrelenting campaign for equal education had helped pave the way for the first public high school for blacks in Daytona Beach. As with many of her other triumphs over ignorance and racial injustice, stirring victories such as this one over the Klan enabled her to deliver a prized message to all black Americans. "We are making progress," she told them.

It was a message that Mary McLeod Bethune worked all her life to fulfill.

Bethune's tireless work in support of social reforms and greater educational opportunities for blacks helped foster racial pride throughout the United States.

## RESEARCH PROJECT

Using your school library or the internet, do some research to find out why African Americans were deprived of the right to vote in the decades after the Civil War. Write a two-page report with your conclusions, and share it with your class.

## TEXT-DEPENDENT QUESTIONS

1. What was the subject of a proposed bill in the 1920 election in Daytona Beach, Florida?
2. What group opposed Mary McLeod Bethune's election canvassing in 1920?
3. How did this group try to intimidate Bethune?

While growing up in a rural area of South Carolina, Mary McLeod spent many long days picking cotton in the fields around her family's farm. Her upbringing instilled in her a strong belief in thriftiness and hard work.

# WORDS TO UNDERSTAND

**leaflet**—a printed sheet of paper that contains information or advertising, and is usually distributed free of charge.

**lynching**—a form of murder that involves hanging the victim; it can be committed by a small group or an angry mob. During the the late nineteenth and early twentieth centuries, thousands of African Americans were lynched without a fair trial.

**scholarship**—a grant or payment made to support a student's education, awarded on the basis of academic or athletic achievement.

**sharecropper**—a tenant farmer in the South who was given credit by the landowner to pay for seeds, tools, living quarters, and food, in exchange for a share of his crop at the time of harvesting.

# CHAPTER 2

# GROWING UP IN SOUTH CAROLINA

Mary Mcleod Bethune was born Mary Jane McLeod on July 10, 1875, in Mayesville, South Carolina. Legend has it that her eyes were wide open when she was born. She would see things before they happened, the midwife who delivered her is said to have told Mary's mother, Patsy McIntosh.

Patsy had been born a slave on the McIntosh farm near Mayesville. According to Mary, her mother was a strong, resourceful woman who "throughout all her bitter years of slavery … managed to preserve a queen-like dignity." It was this regal bearing that attracted Samuel McLeod, who grew up as a slave on the nearby McLeod plantation.

Samuel soon asked his owner for permission to marry Patsy but was told he would first have to buy her. He was lucky to have such a generous owner. Many slaves were not allowed the privilege of choosing their spouses.

Like most slaves, Samuel found it difficult to earn money because he spent most of his day working for his master. Yet in his spare moments he managed to hire himself out to other plantations and farms, picking cotton and husking corn. In time, he earned enough money to purchase Patsy from the neighboring farm and marry her.

Most of the children born to Samuel and Patsy were sold into slavery and lived on nearby plantations. Mary's parents were able to keep track of their children's whereabouts, however, through a secret slave network that sent messages from plantation to plantation. The family was reunited at the McLeod plantation shortly after the Civil War came to an end in 1865.

# A SIMPLE FARM

Mary's family remained on the McLeods' land for several years, until Patsy managed to save up enough money by cooking for her former master to buy 5 acres of hilly farmland 5 miles from Mayesville and 12 miles from the neighboring town of Sumter. On this parcel of land, Samuel and his eldest sons built a log cabin beneath a large oak tree. The cabin had a brick chimney, a solid wood door, and two wooden window shutters. The central room served as the living room, and rooms on each side served as bedrooms for the children. At the front of the cabin was a porch, and at the rear was the kitchen, which had a fireplace for cooking and a brick enclosure for baking. The McLeods named their new lodgings "the Homestead."

Although the farm was simple, the McLeods took great pride in the little they had. A stream by the cabin provided the family with pike, mullet, and eels, and in the woods they hunted rabbits, possum, and quail. Patsy cultivated a vegetable garden, a grapevine, and a fig tree. The children gathered apples and peaches on abandoned plantations, dried the fruit in the sun, and then packed them in sacks to be stored for the winter.

The McLeod children—Mary was the 15th of Samuel and Patsy's 17 offspring and the first to be born at the Homestead—were also expected to work the land

Like the group of South Carolina plantation workers shown here, Samuel and Patsy McLeod were slaves until the end of the Civil War. Many of Mary's brothers and sisters were separated and sold to different owners, but they were reunited as a family when slavery was abolished in 1865.

with their parents. They grew food for the family and cotton as a cash crop. Their day usually began at 5:00 a.m. After having breakfast with their parents, seven or eight of the children headed for the fields.

Like all the McLeods, Mary was a hard worker. Even at a young age she could pick enormous amounts of cotton daily. She usually spent 8 to 10 hours in the field, then went back to the cabin to finish her household chores: adding kerosene to the lamps and trimming their wicks, washing, and helping her mother prepare dinner, including such dishes as hot rice, black-eyed peas, and ham.

After dinner, the entire family gathered around the fire with grandmother Sophia, who sucked on a long-stemmed pipe as she told stories from the Bible and praised God for allowing her to sit by a warm fire with her family, free from slavery. Each night, the McLeods sang hymns, which Mary later used to inspire others.

The McLeods maintained one of the happier homes in the black community of Mayesville, and the Homestead became a regular, welcomed stop for traveling ministers as well as a gathering place for the rural community. Religious services were held beneath the massive oak tree, where birds nested in the clumps of Spanish moss. Sometimes, there was a knock on the door by someone in trouble wanting to know if Patsy, who was very well respected in the community, would speak to the local justice of the peace on their behalf.

Scan here to learn more about Mary McLeod's childhood:

At other times, poor blacks or whites knocked on the door to ask if the McLeods could spare a little food. Mary then followed her mother to where the winter provisions were stored and watched her distribute food she had been saving for the family. Mary was taught at an early age it was better to give to the needy than to keep everything for oneself.

## DISTURBING LESSONS

Mary learned another lesson during her childhood that was just as important but far more disturbing. On one of her birthdays, her father took her to the small town of Mayesville so she could view a horse-and-mule show. Blacks gathered at one end of the ring while whites stood together at the other end. Everyone seemed in good spirits, until a white man who was drunk shoved a match under the nose of a black and ordered him to blow out the flame.

At first, the black ignored this rude intrusion and simply leaned back to avoid the flame. But when the drunk yelled at him again, the black knocked him to the ground—an action that enraged the white crowd. Cries of "String him up!" and "Give me a rope!" quickly filled the air. Samuel grabbed his daughter and joined the other blacks who were rushing away from the **lynching** that was about to take place. "Don't look backward!" Mary was ordered by her father as they left the scene.

Mary noticed that her father was very quiet on their way home. And once they arrived at the Homestead, she was quickly put to bed. Yet she could still hear her parents' concerned, hushed tones in the next room and surmised that something evil had happened to the black man at Mayesville.

As Mary grew older, she began to experience for herself how common it was for blacks to be mistreated by whites. One day, while her mother delivered a load of wash to her former owner, Mary was invited by the owner's grandchildren to play

Samuel and Patsy McLeod saved enough money to buy a small farm after their emancipation. Strongly religious people, they taught their children that God rewards those who have a strong spiritual faith and who work hard in the service of others.

with their dolls and other brand-new toys. Something other than the toys, however, caught Mary's attention: a book.

One of the children saw Mary reach for the book and told her, "Put that down. *You* can't read." This admonishment turned into a challenge for Mary.

In the early 1880s, a number of whites in the South erroneously believed that blacks were inherently unable to read and write. In addition, many southerners were opposed to the education of blacks because they wanted blacks to remain subservient to whites even though they were no longer slaves. Accordingly, there were few schools for blacks in the South at that time.

In 1882, a black educator named Emma Wilson founded a mission school for black children at the Trinity Presbyterian Church in Mayesville. Mary began to attend the school when she was seven years old. She arrived each day after a five-mile walk, wearing copper-toed shoes, a sunbonnet, and a thin, well-worn shawl. She carried with her a lunch of bread and milk in a pail. At the school, she studied reading, writing, arithmetic, and the Bible. She graduated from the mission school in 1886.

# THE VALUE OF EDUCATION

Because Mary knew how to add and subtract, she proved to be an asset to the rural community. When her father took a crop of cotton to the gin, she stood near the scales and corrected the figures cited by the man at the gin, who had most likely been cheating the McLeods for many years. Before long, poor blacks and whites came to her with their sums, which usually concerned the weight of their cotton and the price they were getting for it, or the amount they owed at the village store. **Sharecroppers**—farmers who worked the land of others and accepted a share of what they grew as payment—also wanted to know if they were getting a fair percentage for their work.

"From the first, I made my learning, what little it was, useful everyway I could," Mary later said. Yet she was unable to continue her studies, for there were no other schools nearby. So she returned once again to working in the cotton fields.

When Mary was 12 years old, her parents took her to Sumter to hear the Reverend J. W. E. Bowen of Atlanta, Georgia, speak about his missionary work in Africa. He called for missionaries to go to Africa to bring religion to the natives and raise their quality of life. Although blacks in America had endured slavery and discrimination, they still felt that they were better off than most blacks in Africa. Like Emma Wilson and her mission school, the Reverend Bowen so impressed Mary that she decided to become a missionary.

A year after Mary's graduation from the mission school, Emma Wilson visited her at the Homestead. Mary's former teacher told her that Mary Chrissman, a teacher and seamstress from Denver, Colorado, had been deeply impressed by the reports of Wilson's work that had appeared in **leaflets** sent out by the Presbyterian Board of Missions, an institution that offered spiritual and academic instruction to blacks. Chrissman had decided to offer a small **scholarship** so that some lucky pupil could continue her studies.

The scholarship, it was quickly decided, was to be awarded to Mary Jane McLeod, the most eager of the Mayesville mission school pupils. She was to continue her studies at the Scotia Seminary (now known as Barber-Scotia College) for black women in Concord, North Carolina, where Wilson herself had been trained.

Excitement over the scholarship mobilized the small community where Mary lived. The McLeods worried that they could not provide their daughter with enough clothing and supplies for her schooling, but some generous neighbors presented Mary with newly knit stockings and crocheted collars, and the McLeods' former owners donated dresses that Patsy tailored to fit Mary. A small black trunk was purchased to hold Mary's new possessions.

On an autumn afternoon in 1887, the entire rural community stopped working and headed toward the Mayesville railroad station to say good-bye to Mary. Some

Mary McLeod Bethune was born in this Mayesville, South Carolina, cabin in 1875.

traveled by ox, some by horse and cart, and others walked for miles. At the station, they all gave Mary a hearty send-off as she boarded the train for North Carolina to continue her schooling and learn more about the world.

"Let us help those who help themselves"

# "Found Her Africa at Her Own Door"

EMMA J. WILSON
THE FOUNDER

## MAYESVILLE INDUSTRIAL INSTITUTE

MAYESVILLE, S. C.

In 1882, missionary Emma Wilson began a school for black children in Mayesville, South Carolina, a few miles from the McLeod farm. Mary's parents immediately enrolled her in the school, which eventually grew from a small elementary school into a well-respected vocational institute.

# RESEARCH PROJECT

Sharecropping was a system of farming that became common throughout the South in the years after the Civil War, when newly freed slaves had no way to earn money to support their families and plantation families still owned large tracts of land but had no slaves to provide the necessary labor to operate them efficiently. Using the internet or your school library, do some research on the sharecropping system. What were some of the benefits to sharecropping for former slaves? What were some of the drawbacks? Write a one-page paper.

# TEXT-DEPENDENT QUESTIONS

1. Who were Mary McLeod Bethune's parents?
2. What was the name of Mary's childhood home in South Carolina?
3. How did Mary's education help to keep others from cheating her family?

Scotia Seminary in Concord, North Carolina, as it appeared in the 1890s. Mary's outstanding academic performance earned her a scholarship to study at this school for black women.

# WORDS TO UNDERSTAND

Jim Crow laws—these were laws passed to enforce segregation based on race. They allowed for separate schools, public transportation, restaurants, and more based on race.

segregation—the separation of people in their daily lives based on race.

tenement—a run-down, overcrowded apartment building.

# CHAPTER 3

# DREAMS OF A YOUNG SCHOLAR

Only twelve years old when she arrived at the Scotia Seminary in the fall of 1887, Mary was immediately impressed by what to her were elegant surroundings. The seminary's main building had glass windows and a central staircase. Tablecloths and cutlery were on the tables during meals.

Mary took remedial courses in some basic subjects before she started to attend regular classes. The seminary's faculty, made up of both blacks and whites, provided her with her first example of interracial cooperation. "The white teachers," she later said, "taught that the color of a person's skin has nothing to do with his brains, and that color, caste, or class distinctions are an evil thing." She would draw on her educational experience at Scotia throughout her life, urging both races to work together to fight discrimination.

Mary's tuition fees were covered by her scholarship, but she had to pay for her room and board with her own money. She earned her keep by cleaning the school and doing laundry, undertaking these chores with zeal. She was well aware that her quest for learning demanded that she apply herself with as much determination as she could muster.

When her first year in school ended, Mary did not have enough money to pay for a trip back home to South Carolina. Her family did not have enough money to pay her way, either. Their mule had died, and her father had to mortgage the Homestead so he could buy another animal.

Instead of going home for the summer, Mary worked as a household servant. During the following summers, she worked as a cook, chambermaid, and laundress for families in Pennsylvania and Virginia. Five years passed before she was able to save enough money to see her family again.

## MOVE TO THE CITY

By 1890, when she was promoted to Scotia's normal and scientific course (which corresponds to a present-day junior college), Mary was training to become a teacher. Her best subject was English, and she also excelled in music; she had a wonderful singing voice. However, her studies were secondary to her ultimate goal, which was to become a missionary.

Shortly before Mary graduated from Scotia in 1894, she sent a letter of application to the mission school of the Moody Bible Institute in Chicago, Illinois. She told them, "It is … my greatest desire to enter your Institute for the purpose of receiving Biblical training in order that I may be fully prepared for the great work which I trust I may be called to do in dark Africa. To be an earnest missionary is the ambition of my life." The institute awarded her a scholarship, and she went to Chicago in July 1894 to begin her Bible studies.

Mary quickly adapted to life in the big city. She had little difficulty in dealing with the fact that she was the only black among a thousand students at the institute. "At Moody, we learned to look upon a man as a man, not as a Caucasian or Negro,"

After completing her formal education in 1894, Mary moved to Chicago, where she attended a bible school and did relief work in the city's slum areas. While there, she also pursued her dream of becoming a missionary in Africa. This colored postcard shows a view of State Street in Chicago, circa 1900.

To learn more about Dwight L. Moody, founder of the Moody Bible Institute, scan here:

she later said. "A love for the whole human family entered my soul and remains with me, thank God, to this day."

Mary spread this sense of fellowship by visiting local police stations and singing to the prisoners, trying to comfort them with her inspirational songs. She also worked at the Pacific Garden Mission, where she served lunch to the homeless, and she visited Chicago's southside slums to counsel the needy in their **tenement** apartments.

One particular day of mission work in the slums almost turned into a nightmare. After Mary tried to comfort a woman whose child had recently died and an elderly man who was nearly blind, she knocked by accident on the door of a brothel and was ushered inside. When she introduced herself as a worker from the Moody Institute, she was immediately ridiculed by the people in the room. They asked her to have a drink. She offered to read to them from the Bible instead.

Someone locked the door while Mary was reading from the Scriptures. When she tried to leave, they would not let her. They were planning on having a little fun with her, they told her. She simply sat down and waited until nightfall, when they let her go. She later hinted at her strong religious faith by maintaining, "I wasn't afraid. I knew I had protection."

In addition to helping Chicago's poor and needy, Mary also joined the Moody students on a trip to the northern and midwestern United States to establish Sunday schools. Some of the people whom they encountered had never seen a black before. When a young girl looked at Mary's skin and thought it was dark because it was dirty, the budding missionary pointed to a nearby vase of flowers and told the girl, "Look at all the different colors.… God made man just the way he made flowers. Some one color, some another, so that when they are gathered together they make a beautiful bouquet."

Just before Mary took her final exams in 1895, she received word that the Homestead had burned down. She sent home her savings, which consisted of $40 she had just earned from her first professional singing engagement, and promised to help her family as much as she could. More setbacks were to follow, however. She went to New York City after graduating from Moody in 1895 to ask the Presbyterian Board of Missions for an assignment in Africa. Their answer, according to Mary, was "the greatest disappointment of my life." There were no openings in Africa for black missionaries.

## STARTING A TEACHING CAREER

Mary returned to Mayesville and became Emma Wilson's assistant at the mission school. A year later, she obtained a teaching position at the Haines Normal and Industrial Institute in Augusta, Georgia. The Haines Institute had been started by the visionary black educator Lucy Laney, who in 1873 was a member of the first class to graduate from Atlanta University, one of nearly a dozen black colleges then in existence. Laney opened her school for black children in Augusta after teaching for 12 years in Georgia's public schools.

The Haines Institute was originally located in a church basement among the city's shacks and unpaved streets because black schools did not receive a fair share of public education funds. Laney managed to build the brick school building where Mary began teaching eighth graders in 1896 only after receiving funds from the Presbyterian Board of Missions. Teachers funded by this educational board were required to give lessons in personal hygiene and self-respect as well as in academics.

Laney's accomplishments fired Mary's imagination of what she herself could achieve. Laney had not only demonstrated how to build a school on faith and hard work, but she also showed how important it was to educate young girls. Mary soon realized "that Africans in America needed Christ and school just as much as Negroes in Africa.… My life work lay not in Africa but in my own country." She decided to commit herself to improving the education of young black Americans. Perhaps one day she would even start her own school.

One of Mary's duties at the Haines Institute was to organize the Sunday school program. Yet her classes were not like those at other Sunday schools. Under Mary's supervision, the students went to the nearby shacks and gave baths to the local children. The students also distributed clothing (donated by churches in the North) as well as soap, toothbrushes, combs, and towels. Mary's Sunday school program became a great success, with its attendance reaching 1,000 students.

After Mary had spent a year at the Haines Institute, the Presbyterian Board of Missions transferred her to the Kindell Institute in Sumter, South Carolina, near her hometown of Mayesville. She sent her entire salary home to cover tuition expenses for her two younger sisters, who were studying at Scotia, and to help her parents pay off their debts. In exchange for her salary, Mary's family sent her food.

A gifted soprano, Mary joined the choir of the local Presbyterian church while she was teaching in Sumter. One day during choir practice, she met a handsome teacher named Albertus Bethune who soon proposed to her. They were married in May 1898.

In 1896, Bethune accepted a teaching position at the Haines Institute, a black vocational school in Augusta, Georgia.

The Bethunes' first home was in Savannah, Georgia; Albertus had landed a job there as a teacher. Shortly after they arrived, the couple decided that Mary should also find a teaching post—to supplement Albertus's salary, for black teachers were not paid very well. However, they soon discovered that Mary was pregnant, and she had to stop teaching. Albertus promptly quit his post and started to sell menswear with the hope that his new job would prove to be more lucrative than teaching.

On February 3, 1899, Mary gave birth to the couple's only child, Albertus McLeod Bethune. Six months after Albertus, Jr., was born, the pastor of a Presbyterian church in Palatka, Florida, asked Mary to join the staff of his church's parochial school; he

Inspired by the work of Lucy Laney, the founder of the Haines Institute, Bethune decided to devote herself to creating greater educational opportunities for black students. Most of the black schools then in existence, including the one-room school in South Carolina that is pictured here, were founded by church missionary groups.

had heard of Mary's great success at the Haines Institute. Although Mary's husband was not as excited by the need for black education as she was, he encouraged her to accept the assignment at Palatka.

Mary organized a Sunday school program in Palatka, just as she had done at Haines and Kindell. She also sang to prisoners at the jails every week, and she began what would be a part-time occupation for the rest of her life: selling insurance policies for the Afro-American Life Insurance Company. As the Palatka school began to expand and more teachers were hired, she began to think once more about heading a school by herself.

# A NEW OPPORTUNITY

In 1904, news reached Mary that construction was under way on the Florida East Coast Railway. She realized that a golden opportunity to open a school had arrived. Black laborers from all over the South were gathering in Daytona Beach, 50 miles from Palatka, to begin working on the railroad, and their children would need an education. When time permitted it, Mary looked into the possibility of founding a school and was told that she would probably be able to depend on the growing number of wealthy winter residents in Daytona Beach for support, just as other backers had helped out Lucy Laney.

Mary and her son boarded a train that took them over the Saint Johns River and down the Atlantic coast to Daytona Beach. They sat in the car reserved for blacks under **Jim Crow laws**, which enforced racial **segregation** after the Civil War by requiring separate public facilities for blacks and whites. The rest of the train was filled with white vacationers from the North heading toward Florida's resort towns, among them Palm Beach and Miami.

On her way to Daytona Beach, Mary saw construction gangs of black migrants working on the train tracks. She also saw ragged black children playing on dirt roads while their mothers did the wash. She noticed that all of the rural towns looked alike: Each town had a white section and a black section. However, the black section was always the more impoverished of the two.

When Mary and Albertus, Jr., reached Daytona Beach, they strolled by the glistening Halifax River, which was lined with palmettos and oaks thick with Spanish moss. Then they made their way toward the poor side of town—the black section of Daytona Beach—where she hoped to establish her school. "I found there," she later said, "dense ignorance and meager educational facilities, racial prejudice of the most violent type—crime and violence."

Several nights after Mary arrived in Daytona Beach, she had a dream in which she crossed a river that appeared to be the Halifax. As soon as she made it safely to

In the late 1880s, construction began on a railroad route down the east coast of Florida to the Florida Keys. By 1904, thousands of blacks seeking construction jobs had arrived in Daytona Beach. Bethune visited the area to investigate the possibility of starting a school for the children of the black railroad workers.

the opposite bank, a man rode up to her on a horse. He was Booker T. Washington, the country's leading black educator.

Washington took a soiled hankerchief from his pocket to wipe the sweat from his brow. Then he produced a glittering diamond and handed it to Mary. "This is for your school," he told her.

Mary could see things before they happened, it had once been said. And now, in Daytona Beach, it seemed that her dreams were coming true.

# RESEARCH PROJECT

Using your school library or the internet, do some research to find out more about the system of racial segregation implemented in the Southern states through Jim Crow laws and Black Codes during the decades after the Civil War. Write a two-page report with your conclusions, and share it with your class.

# TEXT-DEPENDENT QUESTIONS

1. What school in Chicago offered Mary McLeod a scholarship?
2. Who was Lucy Laney?
3. Where did Albert and Mary Bethune live after their marriage in May 1898?

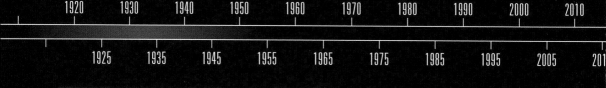

Mary McLeod Bethune's dream of founding her own school came true in 1904, when she rented a cottage and opened the Daytona Normal and Industrial Institute for Negro Girls. She is pictured with a group of her students, circa 1910.

# WORDS TO UNDERSTAND

**illiteracy**—the inability to read or write.

**industrious**—diligent and hard-working.

**spiritual**—a religious song that developed among slave communities in the southern United States, which blends Christian beliefs with African rhythms and influences.

# CHAPTER 4

# THE DAYTONA NORMAL AND INDUSTRIAL INSTITUTE

O n the Morning of October 4, 1904, Mary McLeod Bethune rang a nickel-plated bell to signal the opening of her school, the Daytona Normal and Industrial Institute for Negro Girls. The schoolhouse was a two-story cottage near the railroad tracks. The rent for the cottage was $11.00 a month, but all Bethune could afford at the start was a down payment of $1.50, which was all the money she had in the world.

The school opened with five girls, aged eight to twelve, as the only pupils. Their tuition was 50 cents per week. As time passed and the school accepted more and more students—including boys—some of them boarded with Bethune when their mothers, who worked as maids, went away with their employers for the summer holiday season. This caused Bethune's grocery bills to increase in size and added to her financial worries.

Drawing from the experience of growing up in a poor, rural community where everyone lent a helping hand, Bethune turned to Daytona Beach's black community for assistance. Volunteers cooked and sold chicken dinners and then donated the proceeds to the school. Local fishermen gave part of their day's catch for school meals. Orange growers passed on to the school a portion of their crop.

What was not donated to the school, the **industrious** Bethune made or supplied herself. She used pieces of charred wood for chalk. Mattresses for the boarders were made from corn sacks that were sewn together and stuffed with Spanish moss that had been boiled and dried in the Florida sun. Ink was made from elderberries. According to Bethune, "I begged strangers for a broom, a lamp, a bit of cretonne [a strong cotton cloth] to put around the packing case which served as my desk. I haunted the city dump and trash piles behind hotels, retrieving discarded linen, and kitchenware, cracked dishes, broken chairs, pieces of old lumber. Everything was scoured and mended."

Bethune could be seen walking briskly along the railroad tracks every morning without fail, selling sweet potato pies she had baked the night before. No matter whether she was speaking at a church or riding around town on her bicycle, she never missed an opportunity to tell people about her school. "This is a new kind of school," she would say. "I am going to teach my girls crafts and homemaking. I am going to teach them to earn a living. They will be trained in head, hand and heart: Their heads to think, their hands to work, and their hearts to have faith."

## BARRIERS TO EDUCATION

Bethune encountered many objections—from blacks as well as from whites—to the prospect of education for black children. Whites worried that their black servants would not be content to work for their usual low wages if they knew how to read and write; blacks believed that education would mean reprisals from hostile vigilante groups such as the Ku Klux Klan. Bethune had never received a threat of reprisal during her years as a student and a teacher, but her situation was not a typical one. Entire rural black communities in the South were often terrorized because they dared to build their own school or keep a few books in their log cabins and shacks, even though they were legally entitled to do so.

Blacks in the South were widely discriminated against in other areas besides education. Jim Crow laws made it illegal for them to attend the same churches, schools, restaurants, and theaters as whites. Blacks were not allowed to sit next to whites on public transportation, nor were they permitted to occupy the same hospitals, prisons, orphanages, funeral homes, and cemeteries as whites.

The curriculum of the Daytona Institute was similar to that of the Tuskegee Institute, shown here, which trained students in both academic subjects and industrial skills, such as weaving.

States were legally responsible for providing "separate but equal" facilities for blacks whenever such establishments already existed for whites. But this requirement

Haitian ruler Henri Christophe was one of the black heroes whom Bethune discussed in history classes. Her courses taught students to be proud of the significant contributions that blacks made to the African and American cultures.

usually led to either inferior facilities for blacks or no facilities at all. The "separate but equal" policy also created a potentially life-threatening situation for those who broke the color line, no matter how inadvertently they did so.

Segregated public schools were just one of the many institutions established under Jim Crow laws. Most of the public funds that each state in the South earmarked for education went to schools for whites; nearly all of the black schools had to rely on charitable contributions from supporters. These contributions generally added up to one-tenth of the money that was spent on a school for whites.

When Bethune first arrived in Daytona Beach, the only black school in the area was a kindergarten run by a group of wealthy women. Known as the Palmetto Club, the group had established the kindergarten for the children of their maids. The club members were among the first people in Daytona Beach to welcome Bethune and support her work.

# ORGANIZING ACTIVITIES

Bethune realized that her mission as an educator lay not only in financing and maintaining her school but also in battling the hardship faced by the black community. One way in which she attempted to help the blacks in town was through music. She formed a singing group with her students along the lines of the popular Fisk Jubilee Singers from Fisk University in Nashville, Tennessee.

The group started out by singing on street corners, extolling the virtues of black pride and their faith in God to those who gathered around to listen. Bethune accompanied her students on a small foot-pedal organ as they sang such hymns as "Get You Ready—There's a Meeting Tonight," "Swing Low," "We Are Climbing Jacob's Ladder," and other **spirituals**. Once the group became firmly established, it periodically toured the North to raise money for the school.

Bethune organized other activities as well. Every Sunday, she hosted a gathering of the Loyal Temperance League to talk about the evils of alcohol. During these meetings, she also spoke on the contributions to civilization that had been made by all blacks, including the great African kings. One of her favorite subjects was Henri Christophe, the black king of Haiti, who led a successful revolt against his white colonial rulers and helped establish the world's first black republic. Bethune strongly identified with Christophe's message to his people, "I will teach pride if my teaching breaks every back in my kingdom." A knowledge of black history, she believed, would elevate the pride and ambition of all black Americans.

As Bethune's status in the community grew, the Daytona Normal and Industrial Institute prospered as well. The school began to offer evening classes for adults and special counseling courses for married couples. Bethune lectured the adults about responsibility and family duty in addition to teaching them reading and writing skills. She was sometimes assisted in her efforts by her husband, who helped out when he was not working as a horse-and-buggy driver.

Whenever the community's demands on the school increased, Bethune sought to meet those demands. "In less than two years I had 250 pupils," she said. "In desperation I hired a large hall next to my original cottage, and used it as a dormitory and classroom." The heavy workload was shared by volunteers as well as by a few regular teachers. Their help allowed Bethune to concentrate, she said, "more and more on the girls, as I felt that they especially were hampered by lack of educational opportunities."

## BUILDING A NEW FACILITY

Anxious to see her efforts succeed, Bethune gave every penny that she could spare to the school. She said, "I wore old clothes sent to me by the mission boards, recut and redesigned for me in our dress-making classes." She went so far as to put

Faith Hall was the first building to be erected on the site of the former dump that Bethune and her students transformed into a college campus. The mottoes "Enter to Learn" and "Depart to Serve" were engraved over the main entrance to the hall, and the motto, "Cease to be a drudge; Seek to be an artist" appeared on the wall of the home economics classroom.

Business magnate James N. Gamble, the son of a founder of the Proctor and Gamble company, contributed most of the money required for the construction of one of the Daytona Institute's first buildings. Much of the funding for the school came from wealthy northerners such as Gamble, who vacations in Florida during the winter.

cardboard in her shoes when their soles had worn thin rather than spend money on a new pair of shoes.

Despite Bethune's thriftiness, the school constantly ran short on supplies and remained overcrowded. And the financial difficulties continued. "I was supposed to keep the balance of funds for my own pocket, but there was never any balance—only a yawning hole," she said. "At last, I saw that our only solution was to stop renting space, and build our own college."

Bethune purchased "Hell's Hole," a nearby piece of land that was being used as a city dump. The owner of the land had offered to sell it to Bethune for $250, but she had convinced him to sell it for much less, with a down payment of only $5. She delivered the down payment in nickels, pennies, and dimes wrapped in a handkerchief—coins she had earned by selling ice cream and sweet potato pies to the workmen on the railroad.

Bethune's students worked at carting away the junk from Hell's Hole during the next few months. When the site finally began to look promising, she tried to raise funds for a new school building by calling on the wealthy employers of members of her adult classes. One of the people with whom she arranged a meeting was business magnate James M. Gamble, the son of one of the founders of Procter & Gamble, a maker of household products.

When Bethune met Gamble at his home, he told her he was surprised at the darkness of her skin; he had assumed that such an energetic organizer could only be white. But Bethune was proud of her color and told him so. Then she talked about her plans for the school and invited Gamble to visit the site.

Upon arriving at the former dumping ground, Gamble did not realize that the group of shacks on the site had been put up by Bethune to serve as a makeshift school. "Where is this school?" he reportedly asked her.

"In my mind and in my soul," she replied.

Impressed by Bethune's directness and drive—an impression enhanced by her powerful physical appearance—Gamble became one of the school's leading supporters as well as the chairman of the school's first board of trustees. The financial backing of Gamble and others enabled Bethune to pay the balance due for the land. After the sale was completed, she erected a sign on the land that read: THE DAYTONA NORMAL AND INDUSTRIAL INSTITUTE FOR THE TRAINING OF NEGRO GIRLS.

Work soon began on a new brick building to house the school. A well was dug for water with which to mix the mortar. Neighbors who brought baskets of sand for the mortar helped lay the foundation of the building. The construction of the upper part of the building went especially slowly because the amount of work done each day depended on how much money was available for paying the construction workers. Some of the workers agreed to exchange their labor for free tuition for themselves or their children.

In October 1907, the Daytona Normal and Industrial Institute for Negro Girls officially moved from the cottage by the railroad tracks to its new site. The main building was christened by the 32-year-old Bethune as Faith Hall (after a similar structure at Scotia) even though it was not yet finished; there was nothing more than an outer shell. Inside the building were a floor of dirt and unplastered walls, with matting from the dump serving as inner doors and partitions. There were only a few glass windows in place.

# FINANCIAL DIFFICULTIES

The school's fiscal woes remained despite its growing enrollment. On several occasions, members of the Palmetto Club covered the school's debts. To Bethune, their donations seemed to arrive with almost miraculous timing.

To make her school a financial success, Bethune looked for support from the entire community. She addressed an audience at one of Daytona Beach's popular hotels with the notion of raising funds for the school after her students had given a song and poetry recital. She told of her early life in the cotton fields of South Carolina

The Tomoka Mission was one of a chain of schools that Bethune established to help the families working a rural labor camps outside Daytona Beach. Many of her students at the institute got their first training as teachers at the missions.

and of her teaching career, which had culminated in the establishment of her own school. She concluded her address, which constantly stressed the importance of education for black women, by saying that she had not come to the hotel to beg for contributions. Rather, she was offering the audience an opportunity to share in the vision of her benefactor, Mary Chrissman. "Invest in a human soul," Bethune told her listeners. "Who knows? It might be a diamond in the rough."

After the contributions had been collected, Bethune counted $150 in donations—the largest sum she had ever received at one time. The audience's enthusiastic response convinced her to approach the other large hotels in Daytona

For a video tour of Mary McLeod Bethune's house, The Retreat, scan here:

Beach to find out if they were interested in sponsoring song and poetry recitals as well. She also produced a leaflet entitled *The Advocate*, featuring the headline "See How They Grow!," which she distributed at each performance. The proceeds from these performances helped Bethune meet the monthly property payments and continue the work on Faith Hall.

Bethune counted only six people in the audience at one exclusive hotel where she was expecting a large crowd to attend her students' show. She gave a rousing talk despite the small size of the crowd, and her efforts were rewarded. As donations were being collected after her speech, a man with gray hair and a beard gave her a $20 bill.

The next day, the man appeared at the school and introduced himself as Thomas H. White of Cleveland, Ohio. He requested that Bethune take him on a tour of the school. When he saw the straw matting on the floor of Faith Hall, he asked where it had been taken from and was told that it came from the city dump. When he saw a box of cornmeal and asked if there was anything else to eat, Bethune told him, "That's all we have at the moment."

After inspecting the inside of the building, White walked around the grounds and saw an unfinished building on the school's land. Construction of the building had been stopped because of a lack of funds. "I think the crowning touch," Bethune later said, "was when he saw our dress-making class working with a broken down Singer sewing machine." White was the owner of the White Sewing Machine Company, which was Singer's main competitor.

White brought a new sewing machine to the school on the following day and quickly became a regular visitor to the school. He brought blankets for the students when they were cold and new shoes and a coat for Bethune after hers had become badly worn. He was genuinely interested in the progress of the school and its students.

One day, White arrived at the school with a group of carpenters and plasterers as well as an architect. He was going to pay for these men to finish building Faith Hall, he said. When their work was done, he was going to see to it that the school had plumbing and running water.

Shocked at White's generosity, Bethune tried to thank him. He took her hand in his and said, "I've never invested a dollar that has brought greater returns than the dollars I've given you." He also conspired with Gamble to buy for Bethune a two-story house behind Faith Hall. "The Retreat," as she called it, became her permanent home. When White died nearly seven years later, he left a considerable trust fund for the school.

The school was continually plagued by hardship and impatient creditors even though Bethune received generous contributions. To ease her growing grocery bill, she initiated an agricultural course on the school's grounds to teach her students how to grow food and flowers; vegetables, strawberries, oleanders, and hibiscus were raised and sold to the residents of Daytona Beach. Another project was to enclose the school's grounds and its massive oak trees (much like the one overlooking the Homestead) with a picket fence. This gave the school the appearance of being very well kept.

# BOOKER T. WASHINGTON

Booker T. Washington was born a slave in Franklin County, Virginia, in 1856. He never knew his father. He was raised by his mother in a small log cabin on their master's property, and worked in the fields with other slaves.

When Booker was nine years old, the Civil War ended. Slavery was now illegal. Booker's mother took her children to West Virginia, where she married another former slave. Booker's stepfather promptly put him to work at a salt factory to help support the family. The boy soon taught himself numbers and the alphabet. He had a burning desire to learn to read. But when a small school for black children was started nearby, Booker's stepfather wouldn't allow him to attend. He had to work in the salt factory. Booker persisted, though. Eventually his stepfather agreed to let Booker go to the school if he worked before and after his classes.

For a half dozen years, Booker kept up his studies while working at a series of jobs—in the salt factory, as a coal miner, and as a servant in the home of a wealthy white family. When he was 16, he enrolled at the Hampton Institute, a school for African Americans that was founded in 1868. He excelled there.

After graduating from Hampton, Booker T. Washington worked as a teacher. Then, in 1881, he was named head of a new college in Alabama. The school, called the Tuskegee Institute, prepared African Americans to become teachers. But students at Tuskegee also learned skills such as carpentry, brick making, and farming. In fact, the first Tuskegee students used what they learned to build classrooms and grow food for the college. Washington believed these practical skills were very important. They would help blacks become more self-reliant. They would help blacks lift themselves from poverty.

Washington turned the Tuskegee Institute into one of the top black schools in the country. Many people admired his work there. These included powerful white people, some of whom gave money to Tuskegee. The school grew famous. So did its director.

Washington often spoke out on the issue of race relations. In September 1895, he gave an important speech before a mostly white audience at a trade exposition in Atlanta. In the speech, Washington suggested that southern whites and blacks could live together in a way that would bring prosperity to both races. Whites, he said, should guarantee that black children had access to basic education. Whites should also give blacks economic opportunities. Blacks, in turn, wouldn't insist on political or social equality. They wouldn't demand civil rights. They wouldn't complain about segregation—the practice of keeping the races separate in public places. Blacks would simply work hard. Eventually, Washington believed, they would win the trust and goodwill of the white community. That, and the economic and educational gains made by African Americans, would lead to "progress in the enjoyment of all the privileges that will come to us." Among these "privileges" was equality under the law.

For the most part, whites responded enthusiastically to Washington's Atlanta Compromise speech, as it came to be called. Many African Americans, too, were willing to put off political and social equality in favor of educational and economic progress. For a while, Booker T. Washington was the most prominent leader in the African-American community. But the Atlanta Compromise didn't solve the country's racial problems, and other black leaders soon came to feel that Washington's path of patient cooperation with whites wasn't working.

# A FLOURISHING SCHOOL

Everyone who had supported Bethune from the beginning of her venture—including many of the school's teachers—watched with pride as the school flourished and its students advanced in learning. Among the newer members of the faculty was Frances Keyser, formerly the head of the White Rose Mission for Delinquent Girls in New York City and a highly respected figure in literary circles. Paul Laurence Dunbar, the first black American to gain international recognition as a poet, had asked her more than a decade earlier to critique his manuscript Lyrics of Lowly Life, the poetry collection that ultimately launched his literary career.

One Sunday in 1907, Bethune took a few students on a field trip to an area three miles outside the city. In the area was a camp where migrant workers tapped sap from pine trees to make varnish. Bethune found that the camp was rife with malnutrition, **illiteracy**, and poverty. Without any provisions at hand, she nonetheless decided to offer her assistance. Using a shanty as a makeshift church, she had her students sing for the migrants and their families, and then she gave a short sermon. No one should have to live in such poverty, she told them.

Bethune promised the people in the camp that she would return there every Sunday to read and sing to them. Eventually, she established the Tomoka Mission, where the children of the camp were taught to sing, sew, and play games as well as to read and write, while their parents were counseled on cleanliness, cooking, and sobriety. After the mission was well under way, Bethune left it in charge of some of her students and went on to another camp. Within five years, she had started a chain of missions operating in the turpentine camps in the Florida swamps.

In 1908, the growing male enrollment prompted Bethune to change the school's name to the Daytona Educational Industrial Training School. That same year, the school received an important visitor: Booker T. Washington, who in 1881 had started Tuskegee Institute in Tuskegee, Alabama. Originally consisting of a shanty,

The internationally acclaimed poetry of Paul Laurence Dunbar served as an inspiring example of black achievement to the students at Bethune's school.

a henhouse, a teacher, and 30 students, Tuskegee Institute included more than 60 buildings and hundreds of acres of land by the time its founder came to Daytona Beach to visit Bethune and her school. Washington inspected the school's modest building, livestock, and grounds and then commented, "I don't see how you will ever bridge the chasm between the needs of the school and what you have, but I am sure you somehow will."

Bethune and Washington discussed their respective goals as educators after dinner that evening. Both envisioned an integrated society based on mutual understanding, respect, and tolerance. They both hoped that blacks would someday attain equal rights and be permitted to become leaders in American society, serving as doctors, lawyers, statesmen, scientists, and artists.

But to achieve these positions, blacks first had to be able to support themselves. The students who attended the schools established by Bethune and Washington were taught marketable manual skills that would bring them financial independence. The two educators believed the work they were doing would lay the foundation for all the advances that were to follow.

Whenever Bethune was besieged by worries on educational matters in the years to come, she recalled not only the dream she had about Washington but her subsequent talk with him. Well aware of being entrusted with the future of her students, she was inspired by him to make certain that every "diamond in the rough" would shine.

## RESEARCH PROJECT

Read Booker T. Washington's "Atlanta Compromise" speech, delivered in 1895. (A transcript is available at: http://historymatters.gmu.edu/d/39/). Using the internet or your school library, find out about some other important events in African-American history that occurred during the 1890s, such as increased lynching and violence against blacks, the *Plessy v. Ferguson* Supreme Court decision (1896), and the implementation of new voting restrictions in Louisiana and elsewhere. Write a two-page paper about Washington's speech, and the intended audience, in the context of the decade in which it was written.

## TEXT-DEPENDENT QUESTIONS

1. How many students were in the first class of the Daytona Normal and Industrial Institute for Negro Girls?
2. Why did whites in the South object to the education of black children?
3. What was the Palmetto Club?

| 1920 | 1930 | 1940 | 1950 | 1960 | 1970 | 1980 | 1990 | 2000 | 2010 |
|------|------|------|------|------|------|------|------|------|------|

| 1925 | 1935 | 1945 | 1955 | 1965 | 1975 | 1985 | 1995 | 2005 | 201 |

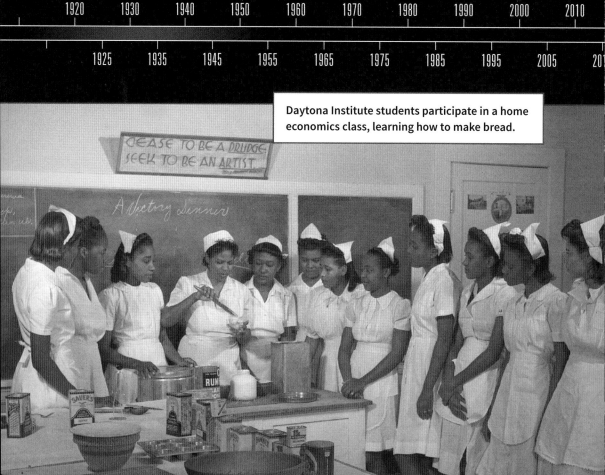

Daytona Institute students participate in a home economics class, learning how to make bread.

# WORDS TO UNDERSTAND

**congregation**—a group of people who assemble regularly, often for religious worship.

**isolation**—to be set apart from other people.

**philanthropist**—a person who seeks to help others, particularly through the donation of large amounts of money.

**picturesque**—visually attractive in a quaint or classic way.

# CHAPTER 5

# CAMPAIGNING FOR EDUCATION

Bethune's relationship with her husband became strained as the Daytona Educational Industrial Training School began to prosper. Not nearly as committed to social reform as his wife, Albertus Bethune believed she was spending too much of her time and energy on trying to help others when she should be devoting herself to her family instead. In 1908, shortly after their son entered his mother's former school, the Haines Institute, Albertus parted from his wife and returned to South Carolina. He died from tuberculosis in 1919 without ever seeing her again.

As Bethune's marriage failed, she became friendly with some of the more influential people who vacationed in Daytona Beach for the winter. She traveled north with them when the winter season came to an end and spread the news of her school to church groups and charitable organizations throughout the country. She continued to make these tours for the rest of her life, describing the hardships endured by southern blacks to audiences who thought of Florida as a **picturesque** place, full of palm trees and beaches.

John D. Rockefeller Sr., one of the wealthiest men in America, was noted for spending large parts of his fortune on charitable causes, including the establishment of a foundation dedicated to support education for black Americans.

Bethune's talks also focused on the urgency of educating blacks. "I have come to the point where I can embrace all humanity—not just the people of my race or another race. I just love people," she maintained. After hearing her speak, few could deny the persuasiveness of her arguments.

During one of her lectures in New York City, Bethune addressed a small but elite audience that included members of some of the country's wealthiest families, among them the Guggenheims and the Vanderbilts. She also visited with **philanthropist** John D. Rockefeller, whom she had met after one of her students' performances at a Florida hotel. Not only had Rockefeller made a contribution to Bethune's school, but he had also given to Bethune his copy of *The Optimist's Good Morning*, a collection of inspirational quotations that she henceforth read from every morning after saying her prayers.

Rockefeller and his heirs paid for the education of Bethune's most promising pupils in the ensuing years. She was doing wonderful work, the senior Rockefeller told her, and should stick to it. "Yes, Mr. Rockefeller," she answered. "All I need is the glue with which to stick." Eventually, the Rockefellers arranged for Bethune's school to receive a sizable grant from the General Education Board, a foundation that the family established in 1902 to support black education.

Yet the finances of the school continued to remain tight despite the growing number of supporters. Bethune insisted on taking in all children regardless of whether or not their parents could afford the tuition, and this strained the school's budget. The continuing expansion of the school was also costly. When the land next to the school was put up for sale, the landowner confided to Bethune that the most interested buyers seemed to be shady characters. His admission spurred Bethune to action. She argued successfully at the next board of trustees meeting that the land had to be purchased; the school had to safeguard the well-being of its students at all costs.

# BUILDING A HOSPITAL

Bethune carried out other types of crusades as well. One of them concerned the need for proper health care for blacks. When one of her female students experienced an attack of acute appendicitis, the girl was refused admittance into the nearest hospital, whose personnel said it served whites only. Bethune desperately pleaded with the white doctor who was in charge of the hospital, and he finally allowed the student to be admitted.

Bethune tried to visit the girl after she had been treated, only to be told by a nurse that blacks were not allowed to enter the hospital through the front door. Incensed by such a policy of discrimination, Bethune marched right past the nurse and discovered that the girl was being neglected by the hospital's staff. She was not in a ward but was confined to a porch behind the kitchen, where she was out of everyone's sight. "Even my toes clenched with rage," Bethune later said about the incident.

Bethune decided to buy a small cottage behind Faith Hall and turn it into a hospital. She began to raise the $5,000 she needed for the hospital by employing the same strategy that she had used to raise funds for the school. She had her students give performances in which they would, she said, "pray up, sing up and talk up." After the first $4,000 had been raised, industrialist Andrew Carnegie donated the balance of the money that was needed.

The hospital was named after Bethune's mother, Patsy McLeod, who died in 1911—the same year the hospital opened. The modest hospital had two beds and a Bible, but before long it was expanded into a 26-bed hospital. T. A. Adams, the only black doctor in town, supervised the staff, which was commended by the city seven years later for its work during a flu epidemic. Bethune ran the hospital until 1927, when she turned over the operation of the institution to the city of Daytona Beach.

Bethune took a rare break from her busy schedule when she attended a conference held annually at the Tuskegee Institute. Booker T. Washington organized these meetings to educate sharecroppers and other farmers in farm management. The conferences were also held to spread the news of the intensive agricultural research being done at Tuskegee.

Bethune, who was usually so busy with fund-raising activities at her own school that she felt **isolated** from the daily affairs of her students, walked around the Tuskegee campus and its buildings constructed from handmade bricks, pleased to see a strong spirit of cooperation there. She especially enjoyed the opportunity to meet with botanist George Washington Carver, who had gained national prominence for his research on the edibility and nutritional and medicinal values of plants—especially the peanut, from which he was able to create more than 300 different products, including washing powder, metal polish, paper, ink, axle grease, and numerous sauces and beverages. When he gave a luncheon at the Tuskegee conference, he served soup, mock chicken, salad, bread, candy and cake, and ice cream and coffee—all derived from the peanut. Both he and Bethune later received honorary degrees from the Tuskegee Institute.

# BUILDING A HIGH SCHOOL

In 1913, the students who had first entered Bethune's school when it was located in a cottage by the railroad tracks graduated from the eighth grade. They were anxious to continue their education, but there was no place for them to study. None of the high schools in the area accepted blacks as students.

Bethune planned on expanding her school to include grades of high school level, but her proposal for a high school had not yet been accredited. Education for

John D. Rockefeller Sr., one of the wealthiest men in America, was noted for spending large parts of his fortune on charitable causes, including the establishment of a foundation dedicated to support education for black Americans.

blacks remained a controversial issue in the South: Some people were strongly opposed to Bethune's plan for a high school, others supported it, and still others—including a local preacher—felt it was not progressive enough. When the preacher saw Bethune in his **congregation** one Sunday, he interrupted his sermon to complain that the school's female students were being taught solely domestic skills that would prepare them only for positions as servants.

# W.E.B. DU BOIS

William Edward Burghardt (W. E. B) Du Bois was born in 1868 in Great Barrington, Massachusetts. He was raised by his mother, who worked as a maid, and by his grandfather. Du Bois attended public school. Almost all his classmates were white, but he didn't experience open racism. He excelled as a student.

After high school, Du Bois went to Fisk University. It was a college for blacks in the southern state of Tennessee. At Fisk, Du Bois first learned about the daily humiliations that many African Americans had to live with. It made him angry. He began writing about the mistreatment of blacks in the school paper.

After graduating from Fisk, Du Bois studied at Harvard University in Massachusetts. Later, he won a scholarship to a university in Germany. There, he learned about the brutal European colonial rule in Africa. It reminded him of the treatment of blacks in the United States.

When he returned from Germany, Du Bois became the first African American awarded a PhD in history from Harvard. He taught at several schools and universities. He wrote about racism and the mistreatment of black Americans.

Du Bois opposed Booker T. Washington's ideas. He argued that African Americans shouldn't wait until white society saw fit to honor their legal rights. Black people shouldn't have to beg for rights other Americans took for granted. Du Bois urged African Americans to be proud of themselves and their culture. He thought that while work was important, education was the key to black empowerment. And he believed that African Americans who were educated—as he was—had a responsibility to fight for those who were not.

In 1905, Du Bois helped start an organization called the Niagara Movement. Its members were leading black intellectuals, activists, and journalists. They weren't interested in the sort of compromises that Booker T. Washington promoted. They strongly condemned racism. They demanded civil rights for African Americans, right away. "We are men!" Du Bois said. "We want to be treated as men. And we shall win."

The Niagara Movement never had more than about 200 members. And by 1910, it had disbanded. Still, it helped pave the way for a larger and more influential civil rights organization. Du Bois cofounded that organization, the National Association for the Advancement of Colored People (NAACP), in 1909. He launched the NAACP's magazine, *The Crisis*. For many years, he served as editor of the publication. In its pages, Du Bois attacked racism and oppression. He refused to apologize for insisting on racial equality. "I am resolved to be quiet and law abiding," Du Bois wrote in *The Crisis* in 1912, "but to refuse to cringe in body or in soul, to resent deliberate insult, and to assert my just rights in the face of wanton aggression."

W. E. B. Du Bois died in 1963. A year later, President Lyndon Johnson signed the Civil Rights Act. It included many of the reforms Du Bois had championed throughout his long life.

Booker T. Washington was the nation's leading black educator in the late 1800s and early 1900s. He believed that blacks would gain economic independence through industrial training. Mary McLeod Bethune agreed with Washington's educational philosophy, but disagreed with the educator on certain social matters.

menial spirit. She adhered to the educational philosophy of Booker T. Washington, who believed that industrial training was the means by which blacks could achieve the economic independence and self-respect that would ultimately win them social and political equality. Ironically, many opponents of racial equality supported industrial training because it helped keep blacks as servants and menial workers.

At times, Bethune showed a willingness to compromise on educational matters, particularly when asking for funds from prospective white contributors (in what she called "begging letters"). Without adequate funding, there was no way she could continue her work. Yet she could be stubborn and uncompromising when important issues were at stake. She felt that in addition to learning trade skills, blacks should try to attain as high an academic level as possible. In this respect, she parted from Washington's views and agreed with his chief critic, educator and author W. E. B. Du Bois, who believed that blacks should be encouraged to make as many gains in society as possible.

The debate over industrial training and higher education intensified for Bethune when she announced her plans to have her school accredited as a high school. Several members of the school's board of trustees suggested that eight grades were more than adequate for black children. Harrison Rhodes, who had originally been brought onto the board to expand the school's fund-raising capabilities and had successfully obtained a large grant for books, was the first to speak on Bethune's behalf. He asked the other white trustees, "Do *your* children have high school education? Then why not *these* children?"

Bethune was shocked by the suggestion that there was no need for a high school. If the board was going to prevent her from starting one, she told the trustees at one meeting, she would start another school from scratch. Then, with her head held high and her eyes flashing, she walked defiantly from the meeting.

That same night, James Gamble, who served as chairman of the board of trustees, called on Bethune at the Retreat and promised to support her effort to start a high school. She soon won her battle with the board, and high school classes began at the Daytona Normal and Industrial Institute. In addition, she established a summer-school program for black women teaching in state schools. Despite their positions as teachers, many of the instructors had not had the opportunity to graduate from high school.

# BATTLING SEGREGATION

More battles were to follow. After the outbreak of World War I in 1914, Bethune was invited to the nation's capital by U.S. Vice President Thomas Marshall to discuss the issue of segregation, especially in relation to the war effort. Both the army and the navy practiced segregation; the American Red Cross relief organization had not yet decided on its policy of black participation. Marshall, who served as president of the Red Cross, wanted to hear Bethune's opinion on the benefits of having a nonsegregated organization.

Bethune was unprepared for the vice president's invitation. She usually wore clothes salvaged from missionary barrels. After fixing up her wardrobe and making a new hat from two old ones, she boarded a train to the nation's capital for her meeting with Marshall.

The vice president was so impressed by Bethune and her commonsense arguments for integration that he sent her on a tour of Maryland, Virginia, and Pennsylvania to talk about the need for blacks to serve in the Red Cross. Largely as a result of her efforts, the Red Cross decided against a policy of segregation. Blacks in the humanitarian organization were allowed to perform the same duties as whites.

Bethune continued to demonstrate her ability as a first-rate, energetic campaigner when she returned to Daytona Beach. Her school's classes and activities were becoming so popular that she was forced to start a drive to raise money for a new dormitory. She called upon her supporters to muster their resources during a

In 1914, Vice President Thomas R. Marshall invited Bethune to air her views on integrating the American branch of the Red Cross. Bethune's subsequent speaking tour proved to be instrumental in getting the organization to change its whites-only policy.

community meeting in Faith Hall, where blacks and whites sat together in flagrant defiance of Florida's color bar. A generous bequest of $80,000 from Flora Curtis, a wealthy New Yorker who wintered in Daytona Beach, enabled construction to begin on a new building, named Curtis Hall. The dormitory was completed in 1922.

Bethune's fund-raising efforts usually did not garner such large bequests. More often, her successful campaigns were the result of tireless devotion to the cause of equal education. She maintained, "I rang doorbells and tackled cold prospects without a lead. I wrote articles for whoever would print them, distributed leaflets, rode interminable miles of dusty roads on my old bicycle, invaded churches, clubs, lodges, chambers of commerce. If a prospect refused to make a contribution I would say, "Thank you for your time." No matter how deep my hurt, I always smiled. I refused to be discouraged, for neither God nor man could use a discouraged soul."

# A VITAL MERGER

For her work to continue as planned, Bethune knew she needed to obtain financial backing that was more secure than the donations from well-wishers. Moreover, this funding would have to come from private sources. She refused to accept state aid when the school was hard-pressed for money; to accept public funds would have placed the school under the control of state legislators, and it would also have subjected the school to segregation laws.

To ensure the school's status as a private institution, Bethune requested funding from the Presbyterian Board of Missions, the same organization that had given Emma Wilson and Lucy Laney their start. After reviewing the situation of the Daytona Educational Industrial Training School, the Board of Missions decided it did not have sufficient funds to support the school. The Catholic church offered its support, but in return it required religious control—a condition that violated Bethune's nondenominational policy.

Bethune then learned from board chairman James Gamble that the Cookman Institute in Jacksonville, Florida, was looking to merge with another school. A school for boys, the Cookman Institute had been founded in 1872 under the Freedmen's Bureau, an organization instituted by the federal government to aid former slaves after the Civil War. The number of students who attended the Cookman Institute was steadily declining, whereas only 100 miles away Bethune's school was bursting at the seams.

A member of the Board of Education of the Methodist Episcopal church suggested to Bethune that the two schools merge, with the Methodist Episcopal church taking over control of the schools' finances and grounds. Although the school would be church-related, it would remain nondenominational, and Bethune would continue to have a strong voice when it came to deciding school policy and conduct.

The merger that took place in 1923 helped save both schools. Yet it saddened Bethune to sign away total financial control of the Daytona Educational Industrial Training School. She had devoted two decades of her life to the school and had

Scan here to learn more about Bethune-Cookman University today:

A group of African-American Red Cross
volunteers in Mississippi, 1920.

transformed it from a shack with a few students into a campus with eight buildings
and a farm, a faculty and staff of 25, and an enrollment of 300 students. As this
important era in her life came to an end, she said: "It is a big thing to yield all. My
feet are sore now, my limbs are tired, my mind weary. I have gone over hills and
valleys, everywhere, begging for nickels and dimes that have paid for this soil, for
these buildings, for this equipment that you find here."

On the day that the newly christened Bethune-Cookman Collegiate Institute
opened its doors, Bethune watched the students walk on the campus sheltered by
the big oaks. Then she gazed at the school's buildings and farm and knew she had
accomplished what she had initially set out to do.

## RESEARCH PROJECT

Using your school library or the internet, find out more about the Bureau of Refugees, Freedmen and Abandoned Lands (commonly known as the Freedmen's Bureau). When was it established, and what was its purpose? What are some ways that the Bureau attempted to fulfill that purpose, and what were obstacles that it faced? Write a two-page report and share it with your class.

## TEXT-DEPENDENT QUESTIONS

1. How did John D. Rockefeller help the Daytona Institute to operate?
2. Who donated $1,000 to ensure that a hospital for blacks could be opened in Daytona?
3. Why did Vice President Thomas Marshall invite Bethune to Washington, D.C., in 1914?

Mary McLeod Bethune in her office at Bethune-Cookman College. As a leading member of a number of civil-rights groups, she worked to unite black women throughout the country.

## WORDS TO UNDERSTAND

barrage—an overwhelming quantity of something, such as criticisms or questions.

economic depression—a sustained period in which economic activity, such as factory production and business sales, are lower than normal. Often, businesses are forced to close or reduce their operations, and many workers are unemployed.

humane—showing compassion or benevolence.

# CHAPTER 6

# INTO POLITICAL LIFE

Bethune's impressive work as an educator led her into the world of politics, where she discovered that she needed to have the patience of a missionary and the tact of a diplomat to get things done. Her future as a political leader was first hinted at in 1909, when she went to Virginia to attend a conference of the National Association of Colored Women during one of her many fund-raising tours. The members of the National Association of Colored Women worked to improve conditions for blacks in the United States, and its conference marked the first time Bethune encountered a group of women whose ambitions to secure equal standing for the black race matched her own.

During the conference, social reformer and educator Mary Church Terrell, the president of the National Association of Colored Women, introduced Bethune by announcing to the membership, "We have a young woman who is building a school in Florida for Negro girls." Bethune then stood up and gave such an impassioned speech about her life's work that political reformer Margaret Murray Washington offered to take up a collection for the school. Madame C. J. Walker, a nationally successsful cosmetics entrepreneur, also volunteered to direct a fund-raising campaign for Bethune's cause. No one was more impressed by Bethune's speech, however, than Terrell. She exclaimed to the group, "Did you hear what came from the lips of that

# BLACK WOMEN'S CLUB MOVEMENT

Numerous black women's clubs formed during the late nineteenth and early twentieth centuries. Some were social clubs. Others were professional clubs or church groups. These groups worked for various causes. Some focused on improving education in the black community. Others sought to improve conditions for women. Still others worked to win women the right to vote. (Women would not achieve that right until August 1920, when the Nineteenth Amendment was ratified.)

Women's clubs gained political power when they joined together. Josephine St. Pierre Ruffin (1842–1924) is credited with organizing the first national convention of black women's clubs. "Our woman's movement is a woman's movement in that it is led and directed by women," Ruffin said at the 1895 Boston meeting. That convention led to the formation of a national organization.

In 1896 activists Ida B. Wells-Barnett, Mary Church Terrell, and Frances Ellen Watkins Harper helped form the National Association of Colored Women (NACW). This group worked to promote suffrage for women. It also campaigned against lynching. And it opposed Jim Crow laws.

Mary Church Terrell served as the first president of the National Association of Colored Women. Other founders included Margaret Murray Washington, Fanny Jackson Coppin, Charlotte Forten Grimké, and Harriet Tubman. By 1910, the NACW claimed a membership of 50,000. It was later known as the National Council of Negro Women.

Educator Mary Church Terrell was the first president of the National Association of Colored Women. Her lifelong battle against racial discrimination was capped in 1954, when she led a successful effort to abolish segregation laws in her home district of Washington, D.C.

Lady Nancy Astor, the first woman member of the
British parliament, welcomed Bethune to England
during her European tour in 1927.

young woman? Someday she will be the president of the National Association of Colored Women!"

True to Terrell's word, Bethune quickly rose to a prominent position in several black women's clubs. In 1917, she became president of the Florida Federation of Colored Women and remained in the post until 1924. In 1920, she founded and was made president of a regional association that later became known as the Southeastern Federation of Colored Women, uniting many of the black women's clubs active in the National Association of Colored Women. During a meeting of the Southeastern Federation of Colored Women in Daytona Beach, Bethune and women from 14 states drew up a program to combat segregation in southern schools and the lack of health facilities for black children. "I have unselfishly given my best," she later said, "and I thank God that I have lived long enough to see the fruits from it."

In 1924, Bethune fulfilled Terrell's prediction by becoming president of the National Association of Colored Women. It was the highest national office to which a black woman could aspire at that time. The organization, drawing on Bethune's seasoned fundraising talents, eventually purchased a building in Washington, D.C., to serve as its headquarters.

During Bethune's tenure as president of the National Association of Colored Women, the organization's membership lobbied for a federal anti-lynching bill and for prison reform and offered job training for women by teaching them to become typists and clerks. While aiding women in rural and industrial areas, the membership also strove to improve the status of women in the Philippines, Puerto Rico, Haiti, and Africa. Bethune, who worked aggressively to project a positive image of black women to whites, insisted the members of the National Association of Colored Women become extremely active politically. Like Lucy Laney, she believed the nation's black women would be the "steady, uplifting and cleansing influence" in the struggle to gain civil rights for all black Americans.

# FOREIGN TRIP

By the summer of 1927, with the Bethune-Cookman College well on its way to becoming a fully accredited liberal-arts college, Bethune was treated by her friends to her first vacation ever, a trip overseas. As president of the National Association of Colored Women and vice-president of the National Council of Women of the U.S.A., an organization affiliated with the National Association of Colored Women since 1899, she was eagerly received abroad. Pope Pius XI granted her an audience at the Vatican, and a number of Europe's leading women befriended her, including Lady Nancy Astor, the first woman to become a member of the British Parliament, and Lady Edith McLeod, who entertained her in Scotland and traced the genealogy of the family name of McLeod, which was common to Scottish-born slave owners.

Bethune was graciously welcomed and entertained throughout her travels in the British Isles—except for one occasion, when a party of white Americans in a restaurant became visibly upset that a black woman was dining in the same room. The people complained to the restaurant owner about Bethune's presence, pointing out that unsegregated seating was not customary in the United States. They were informed what American customs were not necessarily followed all over the world.

Bethune gave a talk on the accomplishments of women abroad shortly after she returned to the United States in October 1927. She insisted that no other group of women in the world had made greater advancements than American women. Accordingly, black American women should not feel they were the only ones to endure hardship; oppression was occurring throughout the world. Her observations in Europe prompted her to say, "I would not change whatever I am for any other that I have seen."

Bethune's faith in herself was reaffirmed when she was invited to a luncheon at the New York City home of Franklin Delano Roosevelt, then the governor of New York. The affair was hosted by Roosevelt's wife, Eleanor, for 35 representatives of

Mary McLeod Bethune (left) is congratulated during a ceremony marking the opening of a new building on the Bethune-Cookman campus. In the center is Eleanor Roosevelt, whom Bethune befriended in 1927. An ardent supporter of civil rights reforms, Roosevelt fought to advance black causes after her husband, Franklin D. Roosevelt, was elected president of the United States in 1932.

the National Council of Women of the U.S.A., Bethune among them. Uncertainty filled the air when the women were called to the dining room. Everyone wondered where Bethune, the only black in attendance, would be seated.

The governor's mother, Sara Delano Roosevelt, promptly took Bethune by the arm and led her to a seat next to the hostess. It was a **humane** gesture that not only marked the beginning of a friendship between the governor's mother and

## THE NAACP

The National Association for the Advancement of Colored People (NAACP) is the country's oldest and largest civil rights organization. Formed more than a century ago, it today boasts more than half a million members.

At the time the NAACP was founded, African Americans were being lynched almost weekly. Race riots were on the rise, even in northern cities. In fact, a race riot that rocked the hometown of Abraham Lincoln helped lead to the establishment of the NAACP. That riot broke out in August 1908. It left at least seven people dead and dozens of black homes and businesses destroyed.

In the wake of the Springfield race riot, a group of concerned whites and blacks met in New York City to discuss what might be done to solve the country's racial problems. W. E. B. Du Bois was one of seven African Americans to attend. The February 1909 meeting led to the formation of the NAACP.

The NAACP's goal was to make sure that all people were protected by the Thirteenth, Fourteenth, and Fifteenth Amendments to the U.S. Constitution. That remains the core mission of the organization. The NAACP works to end racial discrimination. It promotes equal treatment in education, the workplace, and all areas of society.

In 1935, nine young black men known as the Scottsboro Boys were convicted by an all-white jury of raping two white women and were sentenced to long jail terms. Many civil rights groups protested that the boys had been denied a fair trial and lobbied to win their freedom. They are pictured with NAACP officials who were fighting to get a new trial.

Bethune but also led to a deep friendship between Bethune and Eleanor Roosevelt. Bethune's association with powerful political allies such as the Roosevelts proved to be extremely beneficial in the years ahead.

In 1928, the American Red Cross was rewarded for its decision to make Bethune an ally of the relief organization. A hurricane swept through southern Florida, killing more than 1,000 people and leaving many more homeless, and Bethune proved to be a tremendous help in organizing the relief efforts. "I have dealt with epidemics of influenza and other diseases, but I had never been faced with a situation like that," she said. "An effort was made to separate the bodies, but there wasn't time, and the big plows turned over the soil and buried them seven and eight to a grave."

# THE GREAT DEPRESSION

Bethune began to battle an even greater amount of suffering one year later, when the entire country was thrown into a great **economic depression** following the collapse of the New York Stock Exchange in October 1929. Sallie Stewart, who had succeeded Bethune as president of the National Association of Colored Women earlier in the year, advised black women to unpack their best linen and silver. By doing this, they would teach good manners to their children and put up a brave front through the troubled economic period that was to follow.

Stewart's advice seemed totally inappropriate, however, because few women had silver to unpack. According to *The Crisis*, a magazine edited by W. E. B. Du Bois and published by the National Association for the Advancement of Colored People (NAACP), black domestic workers were lining up in New York City to underbid each other in a desperate attempt to get work. Their services were being bargained for by people who normally would not be able to afford domestic workers. There were also many instances in which women worked but did not receive the wages they had been promised, or were not paid any wages at all.

As the nation's economy grew weaker and weaker, the number of unemployed people soared. Black men were particularly victimized by the failing economy. After losing their jobs, they were usually unable to find new ones because out-of-work whites began to accept even the the most menial positions, which in the past had been held by blacks.

Blacks were subsequently forced to rely on the women in the family to be the breadwinners. As Bethune told a meeting of the Chicago Women's Federation, "In recent years, it has become increasingly the case [that] ... the mother is the sole dependence of the home while the father submits unwillingly to enforced idleness and unavoidable unemployment."

Although circumstances were dire for many blacks, a fair number of black women were making substantial gains. By 1930, nearly half the graduates of black colleges were women. Bethune noted that these women had the potential to make a difference in the advancement of their race. She said in an article published in the *New York Age*, a black newspaper, that black women were not only "more numerous and diversified and more keenly alive to the group" than black men who were similarly educated, but they were in a "better position to make use of the Negro's purchasing power as an effective instrument to keep open the doors that have remained closed."

In expressing these ideas, Bethune continued to move away from Booker T. Washington's views on black labor and move closer to the position held by Du Bois, who called for an elite and educated "talented tenth" to provide the nation's blacks with leadership. Washington had said years earlier, "I would much rather see a young colored man graduate from college and go out and start a truck garden, a dairy farm, or conduct a cotton plantation, and thus become a first-hand producer of wealth, rather than a parasite living upon the wealth originally produced by others, seeking uncertain and unsatisfactory livelihood in temporary and questionable positions." Du Bois, on the other hand, believed that blacks should use their newly acquired economic power as leverage in their fight to overcome their secondary status: "One ever feels his two-ness,—an American, a Negro," he said, "two souls, two thoughts, two unreconciled strivings; two warring ideals in one dark body." Du Bois, unlike Washington, could not separate economics from politics, and Bethune refused to do it as well.

# INVOLVEMENT IN NATIONAL ISSUES

Bethune's insistence on looking at the overall picture carried over into other topics. As the early 1930s progressed, she felt the National Association of Colored Women was being overly attentive to regional matters at the expense of issues of greater national importance. Seeking an organization to address these larger issues, she came up with the idea for a council that would oversee all of the national black women's clubs and organizations. The main purpose of this council, she said, was to "work out many problems that face us as a group." The idea had first come to Bethune while she was attending a White House conference on child welfare. She had realized that an organization with so much stature would have greater access to federal funding than individual clubs and organizations.

In December 1935, Bethune formed the National Council of Negro Women. She told Terrell, "The result of such an organization will ... make for unity of opinion among Negro women who must do some thinking on public questions, it will insure cooperation among women in varied lines of endeavor and it will lift the ideals not only of individual organizations, but of the organizations as a group." Bethune became president of the National Council of Negro Women at its inception and remained the head of the organization until 1949.

As the leader of the National Council of Negro Women and a member of the Commission on Interracial Cooperation, an organization formed in 1919 to improve race relations in the South, Bethune was determined to put a stop to the alarming number of lynchings that victimized blacks. Lynchings were usually practiced by white vigilantes who wanted to maintain racial supremacy by terrorizing blacks into remaining in subservient roles. Most of these acts of mob violence took place in the South, where whites were unwilling to accept the rising status of blacks in American society.

For a short video on lynchings in the South, scan here:

Bethune told Will W. Alexander, the president of the Commission on Interracial Cooperation, she planned to enlist the aid of white women in the South to stop the increasing tide of racial violence. A white Methodist minister and leading crusader against racism, Alexander was familiar with Bethune's ways of persuasion. He had witnessed her in action in 1924, at a National Association of Colored Women conference in Memphis, Tennessee.

The atmosphere at that conference, attended by both black women and white women, had been uneasy at first because it was not customary for blacks and whites to sit together in the South. But when the white women at the conference heard the black women speak about the constant **barrage** of prejudice and the fear of violence under which they lived, and then heard them discuss how their children were deprived of education and health care, the mood of the meeting changed. The dividing line between black and white grew fainter as the southern white women realized the heartache black families had to endure.

By the mid-1930s, Bethune was ready to insist that southern white women do what they could to stop racial violence. Her call for action was answered by Jessie

Daniel Ames, who formed the Association of Southern Women for the Prevention of Lynching. The organization grew to 36,000 members by 1936, yet it never wielded the kind of political influence Bethune had hoped it would.

Curiously, the organization remained silent when it was most needed. This proved true in 1935, during the second court battle involving the conviction of the Scottsboro boys—nine black youths in Alabama who were handed lengthy jail terms after an all-white jury found them guilty of raping two white girls in 1931. The court determined that blacks had been systematically excluded from the jury selection process, which violated the Fourteenth Amendment and its guarantee of "equal protection of the laws." A rallying cry against prejudice and violence by the Association of Southern Women for the Prevention of Lynching might have prevented similar injustices from occurring.

The Association of Southern Women for the Prevention of Lynching managed to make some gains—such as helping to achieve better housing conditions for the black community in Dallas, Texas—but controversy more often surrounded the organization, whose all-white membership was accused of shunning blacks. When the organization refused to lobby for a federal anti-lynching bill drafted by the NAACP in 1935, many of the nation's leading black female activists gave up on it. Educator Charlotte Hawkins Brown, the founder and principal of the Palmer Memorial Institute in North Carolina, remarked after the anti-lynching bill was defeated that southern white women could have done more "to bring about… freedom for the Negro race than a million in the north" because southerners were in the majority in Congress.

## CHANGING ATTITUDES

Bethune was disappointed by the lack of effort shown by the Association of Southern Women for the Prevention of Lynching, but she refused to lay blame on anyone. Unlike some other activists, she made it a point never to criticize anyone too severely; she would never know when she might need their support in the future. "I am diplomatic about certain things," she said. "I let people infer a great many things, but I am careful about what I say because I want to do certain things."

Black women's groups became divided over the issue of racial integration around the time that the Association of Southern Women for the Prevention of Lynching proved to be ineffective. Some groups felt blacks should devote themselves to establishing schools, newspapers, churches, and cultural groups that remained separate from white institutions. Other groups wanted to break down the barriers of segregation by forcing white institutions to become integrated.

These conflicting views mirrored what was taking place within the ranks of the country's most influential civil rights organization for black Americans, the NAACP. In 1935, Du Bois resigned from the NAACP and left his position as editor of *The Crisis* because his views differed from those held by Walter White, the organization's executive secretary, who favored integration. The fiercely proud Du Bois, who maintained that black Americans "have not made the slightest impress on the determination of the overwhelming mass of white Americans not to treat Negroes as men," believed they needed to rely on their own institutions to overcome the adversity they faced during the Great Depression.

Like many people, Bethune was torn over this issue because she envisioned an integrated society yet believed that blacks had made the largest gains in organizations and institutions that were not racially integrated. She illustrated this latter point by, saying, "If I touch you with one finger, you will scarcely notice it. If I tap you with two fingers, you will feel a slight pressure, but if I put all my fingers together in a fist, you will feel a mighty blow." As a result, she supported integration but favored the establishment of black organizations and institutions. In effect, she endorsed any position that she felt would advance the cause of equal rights.

Bethune's contributions to the lives of black Americans were formally recognized in 1935. She was named one of the 50 most influential women in America by a group of newspapers and was given the prestigious Spingarn Medal as well. Awarded by the NAACP, the medal was established to honor the "highest or noblest achievement by an American Negro."

After Bethune was honored by the NAACP, she was congratulated for her accomplishments by a number of influential people. Among them was the Reverend Adam Clayton Powell, Sr., the minister of the Abyssinian Baptist Church in the New York City district of Harlem. The district boasted the largest black population in the nation, and Abyssinia had the largest black congregation of any church in the country. "It is a long way from the rice and cotton fields of South Carolina to this distinguished recognition," he told her. "But you have made it in such a short span of years that I'm afraid you are going to be arrested for breaking the speed limit."

## RESEARCH PROJECT

For many black Americans, their already-bleak prospects for earning money were made worse by the Great Depression of the 1930s. Black workers were often the first to be laid off from their jobs, and the unemployment rate of blacks was at least twice as high as the rate for white workers. Using your school library or the internet, find out more about how black Americans were affected by the Great Depression. Write a two-page paper and present it to your class.

## TEXT-DEPENDENT QUESTIONS

1. Who was Mary Church Terrell?
2. Where did Bethune go on vacation in 1927?
3. What was the Association of Southern Women for the Prevention of Lynching?

Mary McLeod Bethune speaks to a group of students on the campus of Bethune-Cookman Institute.

ENTER TO LEARN

# WORDS TO UNDERSTAND

asthma—a respiratory condition that causes breathing problems.

emancipator—a person who frees others from slavery.

peonage— a system in which workers are bound in servitude because of debt.

# CHAPTER 7

# BETHUNE AND THE BLACK BRAIN TRUST

W hile the Great Depression led to poverty and despair in the United States, it was also responsible for increasing the political clout of many black Americans. During the 1930s, nearly a half million blacks left the rural South to look for work in the industrial North. This influx of blacks increased the number of black voters in such urban centers as Chicago and New York and resulted in a strong Democratic party in these cities.

The Republican party believed it had secured the loyalty of black voters simply by being the party of the Great **Emancipator**, Abraham Lincoln, and so it did little to go after the black vote in the 1930s. However, the Democratic party actively recruited black voters in the 1930s. It did so largely through the New Deal, the program developed by President Franklin D. Roosevelt and his Democratic administration to promote economic recovery and bring about social reform. According to *The Crisis*, "The most important contribution of the Roosevelt administration to the age-old color line problem in America has been

President Franklin D. Roosevelt took office in 1933, in the midst of the Great Depression. He instituted a sweeping program of social reforms and relief measures known as the New Deal.

its doctrine that Negroes are part of the country as a whole.... This thought has been driven home in thousands of communities by a thousand specific acts."

White House officials had already made Bethune feel she was "part of the country" by the time Roosevelt became president in 1933. Five years earlier, President Calvin Coolidge had summoned her to the nation's capital to take part in a conference on child welfare. She was then asked to help relay information from federal agencies to people in the South about health care and education.

When Herbert Hoover succeeded Coolidge as president in 1929, Bethune was asked to participate in the National Commission for Child Welfare. As a member of this group, she suggested which black educational institutions should be supported with federal funds. She also became a member of the Hoover Commission on Home Building and Home Ownership. But it was under President Roosevelt's administration that she achieved her greatest influence in the world of politics.

# WORKING FOR THE FEDERAL GOVERNMENT

In 1935, Bethune was appointed by the Roosevelt administration to a position in an agency called the National Youth Administration. A product of the New Deal, the agency was created to combat unemployment among young Americans. The National Youth Administration paid people between the ages of 16 and 24 for participating in relief work and job-training programs.

After the agency had been in existence for a year, Bethune reported to the president that the agency meant a great deal to young blacks. She told him, "We are bringing life and spirit to these many thousands who ... have been living for so long in the alleys and back streets and woods." She also took the opportunity to remind the president that all blacks were looking for him to provide them with leadership. "The further an individual is down, the more chance he may have to come up," she said. "But the Negro cannot find his way to the opportunities that are opening unless he has someone to guide him."

In 1936, Bethune was appointed director of the National Youth Administration's Division of Negro Affairs, and thus became the first black woman to be placed in charge of a federal agency.

Bethune was so successful in convincing Roosevelt of the need for greater leadership that one week later he offered her the post of administrator of the Office of Minority Affairs, a newly created department within the National Youth Administration. In June 1936, the title of the department was changed to the Division of Negro Affairs, and she was assigned the position of director. With this appointment, she became the first black woman to serve as the head of a federal agency.

As a special adviser on black affairs, Bethune joined forces with other prominent blacks who occupied administrative posts in New Deal agencies. Along with Robert Vann, William Hastie, Robert Weaver, Lawrence Oxley, and Frank Home, she formed an informal presidential advisory board known as the "Black Cabinet." This group of federal officials was also referred to as "the Black Brain Trust."

Bethune's fellow Black Cabinet members worked in different fields of government service. Formerly the editor of the *Pittsburgh Courier*, a leading black newspaper, Vann served as a special assistant to the U.S. attorney general. Hastie served as assistant solicitor to the Department of the Interior before becoming the dean of the School of Law at Howard University, the governor of the Virgin Islands, and a judge on the U.S. circuit court of appeals. Weaver, who as secretary of housing and urban development under President Lyndon B. Johnson became the first black member of a president's official cabinet, served in several New Deal agencies, including the Federal Housing Authority. Oxley, a social worker, was chief of the Division of Negro Labor in the Department of Labor. And Horne (the uncle of entertainer Lena Home), had been a poet, physician, and the president of Fort Valley Junior Industrial College in Georgia before serving with several agencies, mostly involving federal housing programs.

The Black Cabinet served as a crucial link between black Americans and the U.S. government, relaying information about federal programs to blacks nationwide and advising government officials on the special needs of black citizens. In her capacity as director of the Division of Negro Affairs, Bethune was frequently able to express to a concerned audience her frustration at the obstacles and racial hostilities often

THE NEW DEAL

The Daily Blackness Presents

Black History Lesson

BLACKNESSMAGAZINE.COM

Scan here to learn how black Americans were helped by Roosevelt's New Deal:

faced by blacks. During a speech to the Association for the Study of Negro Life and History, she said, "Hemmed in by a careless world, vast numbers of us [have] sunk into the degradation of **peonage** and virtual slavery.... About us cling the ever tightening tentacles of poor wages, economic insecurity, sordid homes, labor by women and children, broken homes, ill health, delinquency and crime."

## FIGHTING RACISM

Bethune maintained she could hear blacks "cry out in this awesome darkness" and was determined to help them find a way into the light. Her determination increased when it became clear that the promises made by the Roosevelt administration to promote racial equality in such areas of American life as employment and low-cost housing were not being kept. Many of the white supervisors of federal relief agencies were distributing their relief grants unequally, with the majority of funds going to whites.

This was largely true of the National Youth Administration. The agency's branch in each state was headed by an administrator who was responsible for running the branch's programs and dispensing grants. Each branch administrator was assisted by an advisory committee, which was supposed to reflect a cross-section of people from different occupational and ethnic groups. Yet it was ultimately up to each administrator to select the membership of his advisory committee.

The makeup of these committees became a highly charged issue when administrators in the southern states refused to integrate their advisory committees. In Texas, Lyndon B. Johnson was the state's first National Youth Administration director. He insisted that whites in his state would object to serving on an integrated committee, and so his advisory committee did not include any black members. He was also reluctant to give policy-making positions and supervisory responsibilities to blacks.

Bethune and the Office of Minority Affairs attempted to force Johnson to integrate his advisory committee. Yet other National Youth Administration officials as well as the federal government failed to put sufficient pressure on Johnson. Accordingly, a separate advisory committee made up of blacks was established. This greatly affected how much the Texas branch could accomplish because a second advisory group increased the branch's operating expenses, thereby depleting the branch's budget.

Bethune was not successful in her effort to integrate the state advisory committee in Texas, but she did see to it that several state advisory committees in the South—including those in Alabama, Arkansas, Mississippi, and Georgia—became integrated. She also did her best to channel funding to black schools in the segregated South so their facilities would be more on a par with the facilities at schools attended by white students. She tried to point out the sense of fair play that guided her actions by saying, "You white folks have your swimming pool if you think that best. Just give us one to enjoy too."

As the director of the Division of Negro Affairs, Bethune traveled all over the country to campaign for better and higher education for blacks. She succeeded in

Mary McLeod Bethune achieved her greatest recognition at this Washington, D.C., townhouse, which was the first headquarters of the National Council of Negro Women (NCNW) and was Bethune's last home in Washington, D.C. From here, Bethune and the NCNW spearheaded strategies and developed programs that advanced the interests of African American women. Today the house is a National Historic Site.

getting the National Youth Administration to increase the amount of financial aid given to black youths for training in industry, library science, and mechanical and construction work. Special funding from the agency also made it possible for many black students to continue their education in graduate schools.

Bethune generally used every appropriate contact and resource available in achieving such political victories. When federal funding earmarked for a housing project in Daytona Beach was held back because the money would be used to help blacks instead of whites, she appealed to Eleanor Roosevelt for help. The first lady promptly called the head of the Federal Housing Authority, who immediately ordered that a half million dollars be spent on the housing project for blacks. The city's housing committee made Bethune a member once it realized the extent of her influence, thus making her the first black in Daytona Beach to become a member of a city committee.

In 1940, Bethune became vice president of the NAACP. She insisted that wherever groundbreaking African Americans went, many more blacks would follow. This not only meant gaining positions in federal, state, and municipal agencies, but working in hospitals and other places as well. Even though American medical schools had begun to train blacks as early as 1868, black physicians were not allowed to tend to their patients in white hospitals because of segregation practices.

When Bethune was 65 years old, she suffered so greatly from **asthma** that she needed a sinus operation to help her breathe more easily. She insisted upon entering the medical center at Johns Hopkins University in Baltimore, Maryland, that her black doctors be allowed to attend the operation. Their presence broke a long-standing practice of segregation at one of the country's leading medical institutions.

No matter what station in life people occupied, Bethune always took the time from her busy schedule to impress upon them that they should fight for racial equality. When a white taxi driver in Washington, D.C., waved her away from his cab, she opened the door and sat in the backseat despite his protests. She later said, "I gave him the address of the Department of Labor, 14th and Constitution, and told him if he refused to take me there I would see that his license was withdrawn. He had no answer, but drove off sullenly."

Bethune remained in the cab when the taxi reached her destination and talked with the driver at length about her efforts to win civil rights for blacks. "I did not want him to consider me as an individual, but only as a representative of the American Negro," she said. "I wanted him to get over his prejudice against people because of the color of their skins. I told him his cab was for the conveyance of the public, and that anyone who could pay for his transportation had every right to the use of it."

The driver stared at Bethune when she got out of his taxi. Then he tipped his hat with respect before driving away.

# RESEARCH PROJECT

In 1896, the U.S. Supreme Court ruled in *Plessy v. Ferguson* that public facilities could be segregated, as long as the segregated facilities were equal in quality. Using your school library or the internet, find out more about the *Plessy v. Ferguson* decision. What was the result? Write a two-page paper and share it with your class.

# TEXT-DEPENDENT QUESTIONS

1. Why did African Americans voters join the Democratic Party in the 1930s?
2. What was the Black Brain Trust?
3. Where was Bethune treated for her asthma when she was 65 years old?

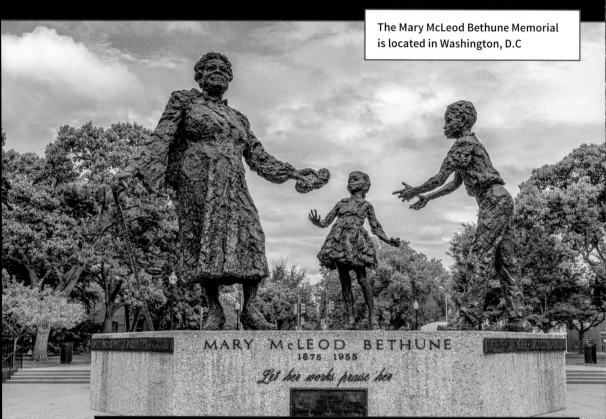

The Mary McLeod Bethune Memorial is located in Washington, D.C

MARY McLEOD BETHUNE
1875 1955
Let her works praise her

# WORDS TO UNDERSTAND

**desegregation**—a process to end racial segregation in public areas.

**unconstitutional**—used to describe legislation or regulations that are not in keeping with the basic principles set forth in the constitution of the United States.

**widow**—a woman whose husband has died, and who has not yet remarried.

# CHAPTER 8

# AN INSPIRING LEGACY

As World War II engulfed most of Europe in 1941, the United States made preparations for entering the war. Bethune urged blacks at the Third National Negro Conference to join the war effort even though they were being openly discriminated against by the armed forces, which practiced racial segregation, and the defense industry, which hired relatively few blacks to work in its factories. She felt a demonstration of patriotism by black Americans might encourage the government to integrate the military and call for fair employment practices in defense industry plants. "We must not fail America," she said at the conference, "and, as Americans, we must insist that America not fail us!"

Nearly a half million blacks trained by the National Youth Administration were granted work in defense industry–related jobs. Yet an equal number of skilled blacks were still looking for work. In addition, millions of unskilled black laborers remained unemployed even though there were jobs in the defense industry and on farms around the country that needed to be filled. No matter how willing and eager black Americans were to find work, racial discrimination stood in their way.

In the spring of 1941, labor leader A. Philip Randolph arranged for blacks from all over the country to participate in a nationwide protest against racial discrimination. A

# A. PHILIP RANDOLPH

Martin Luther King Jr. once called A. Philip Randolph "the conscience of the labor movement." Randolph was an extraordinary activist in the civil rights movement: He served as a labor organizer, journalist, and civil rights leader for much of the twentieth century.

Randolph was born in Central City, Florida, on April 15, 1889. He learned about civil rights at an early age from his father, a preacher committed to the idea of combating racial injustice. Randolph graduated as valedictorian from Cookman Institute and moved to Harlem in 1911. He attended the City College of New York and New York University, supporting himself by working as an elevator operator.

In 1917, Randolph became a cofounder and coeditor of the black socialist magazine *The Messenger.* Eight years later, he founded the first predominantly black labor union, known as the Brotherhood of Sleeping Car Porters. The union quickly became one of the leading forces in both the civil rights and labor movements, striving to improve the working conditions of the railroad's approximately 10,000 black employees.

Randolph worked as a leader and spokesperson for the Brotherhood for several years. By 1941, his focus had expanded to challenge discrimination in the armed forces. He led a march on Washington to protest discrimination in the defense industries. Randolph influenced President Harry Truman's ultimate decision to desegregate the American military in 1948.

Randolph was one of the organizers of the 1963 March on Washington, where Martin Luther King Jr. delivered his "I Have a Dream" speech. He continued to speak out for racial and economic justice and equality until his death on May 16, 1979.

Labor leader A. Philip Randolph was at the forefront of the civil rights struggle from the mid-1920s until the 1960s. He pushed for a march on Washington, D.C., and ultimately was a leader in putting together the 1963 March on Washington for Jobs and Freedom, where Martin Luther King made his "I Have a Dream" speech.

Mary McLeod Bethune walks to Sunday afternoon chapel in January 1943—her last day as president of Bethune-Cookman College.

graduate of the Cookman Institute, he had battled to improve the working conditions of black sleeping-car porters by organizing them into a union in 1925. Twelve years later, he successfully negotiated a working agreement between the union of porters and the Pullman Palace Car Company, one of the largest employers of black labor in America. In subsequent years, he continued to play a leading role in the fight for civil rights.

Randolph, with Bethune as one of his staunchest allies, coordinated what he termed "a thundering march on Washington." He and his supporters made arrangements for more than 100,000 black Americans to descend on the nation's capital and sit on the White House lawn until their demands for equal rights were met by the government. The only way President Roosevelt was able to persuade

Randolph to call off the protest march was by signing an executive order on June 25, 1941, that stated, "There shall be no discrimination in the employment of workers in defense industries or in government because of race, creed, color, or national origin."

# WARTIME ACTIVISM

Six months later, when the United States formally entered World War II, many blacks assumed racial oppression would soon be eliminated in America. Not only had President Roosevelt signed an executive order to stop discrimination, but they saw their country become deeply united against the racist policies of Nazi Germany. Yet segregation continued to exist in the armed forces, and blacks who competed for jobs with whites still faced discrimination.

Amid the ongoing discrimination, Bethune managed to make a number of contributions to the war effort. She was instrumental in establishing the Civilian Pilot Training Program at the Tuskegee Institute, which graduated black aviators who fought in World War II. She was named as an adviser to Secretary of War Henry Stimson on the selection of officer candidates for the Women's Army Auxiliary Corps (WAAC). She was also appointed to the board of directors of the American Woman's Voluntary Services, whose activities ranged from selling war bonds to sponsoring blood-donor campaigns, and she was made a general in the Women's Army for National Defense, another service organization.

Bethune realized that if she wanted to play an even larger part in the battle against segregation in wartime America, she would have to relinquish some of her many duties. In addition to her administrative post with the National Youth Administration, she was still the president of Bethune-Cookman College (which had become a fully accredited college in 1929) and the National Council of Negro Women. She resigned from the college in 1942 after deciding that her countrymen needed her more than anyone else.

The National Youth Administration was nearly abolished in 1942 because wartime defense spending left little funding for social programs. Bethune was still working for the agency when it was finally shut down because of a lack of funding one year later. After seven years of dedicated service as a federal adviser, Bethune came to the end of a chapter in her lifelong effort to help the nation's black youth.

Bethune continued to keep an extremely busy schedule even though she was no longer a government official. She was made a sponsor of the Planned Parenthood Federation of America, served on the board of the National Sharecroppers Fund, worked on a Friends of the Atlanta School of Social Work committee, joined the Americans for Democratic Action, and became honorary chairman of the Harlem Division of the American Committee for Yugoslav Relief. She also went on to write columns for the *Pittsburgh Courier*, *Chicago Defender*, and *Washington Post*.

In addition to these activities, Bethune made many public appearances as a speaker. At New York City's Madison Square Garden, she spoke to the National Council on American-Soviet Friendship, a group that promoted fellowship between the women

MARY
MCLEOD
BETHUNE

Scan here for more information about Mary McLeod Bethune:

of the United States and of Soviet Russia. She said, "I am deeply interested in the urgent needs of *these* people and in having *our* people make some contribution in this area of world rehabilitation."

Because Bethune worked as a social activist for *these* people, rumors spread that she was a communist working in concert with the Soviets. In February 1943, she was formally accused of being a communist by the House Un-American Activities Committee, which investigated Americans whose actions were suspected of running counter to the interests of the U.S. government. Established in 1939, the investigative committee labeled many Americans as subversive simply because they criticized some of the government's policies.

Bethune maintained that she would "continue along the straight, true course I have followed through all these years" after she was charged with being a communist. Newspapers throughout the country rose to her support and printed editorials defending her. Her name was cleared by the investigative committee one month later, thereby enabling President Roosevelt to make her his special adviser on black issues.

One of Bethune's boldest actions as a civil rights activist came in 1944, when she and a number of other prominent black Americans—including A. Philip Randolph, Adam Clayton Powell, Jr. (who was soon elected to Congress), and Thurgood Marshall, the NAACP's special counsel who was later appointed to the Supreme Court—signed a "Declaration by Negro Voters," a proclamation that blacks should not feel bound to a party's political platform. Instead, they should carefully examine the merits of every candidate and vote only for the ones who supported racial justice. Bethune became an active campaigner in Roosevelt's successful bid for a fourth term in office later in the year, indicating that she believed the president was working hard to achieve racial justice.

In April 1945, shortly before World War II officially came to a close, a 50-nation conference was scheduled to meet in San Francisco, California, to draw up plans for

Mary MacLeod Bethune attends a banquet given by the Society for the Advancement of Colored People to honor delegations from the Dominican Republic, Liberia, and Haiti at the San Francisco Conference, May 1945. Representatives from 46 nations came together at the conference to create the United Nations.

the organization that would eventually become the United Nations. Bethune was invited to attend the conference as a delegate from both the National Council of Negro Women and the NAACP. She was in the midst of finalizing her plans to attend the conference when she received word on April 12 that President Roosevelt had died.

Bethune took part in the United Nations conference two weeks after she attended Roosevelt's funeral. When she returned home from the organizational meeting, she found a long, thin package awaiting her. Inside the package was a gnarled oak walking stick. Inscribed on a silver plate inlaid in the wood was "Franklin Delano Roosevelt." The walking stick had been sent by the president's **widow**, Eleanor, who knew Bethune kept a collection of walking sticks as a hobby.

Bethune continued the fight for equal rights after she turned 70 years old, taking on several battles in her hometown. She helped blacks in Daytona Beach win permission to use the municipal beach. She also helped establish a black resort area in the community.

In 1949, Bethune resigned as president of the National Council of Negro Women and traveled to the black republic of Haiti. She had always admired the fortitude and bravery of the Haitian people, who had freed themselves from colonial French rule, and it was apparent that the Haitians admired her in return. They awarded her the country's highest distinction, the Medal of Honor and Merit, making her the first woman to receive this prestigious award.

In 1951, Bethune was appointed by President Harry Truman to serve as a member of the Committee of Twelve for National Defense. The following year, she realized a longtime dream by traveling to Africa. There she visited the nation of Liberia and represented the United States at the third inauguration of Liberia's president, William Tubman. In Liberia, she also spoke at the American embassy, organized a chapter of the National Council of Negro Women, and was awarded the country's Star of Africa medal.

# FINAL YEARS

Bethune was hospitalized for a heart ailment after she returned to the United States. But even though her health was beginning to fail, she took one more trip abroad. In the summer of 1954, she went to Caux, Switzerland, to attend an international peace conference, the World Assembly for Moral Rearmament.

During the last years of her life, Bethune continued to participate in numerous organizations despite her poor health. Among them were the Mary McLeod Bethune Foundation, the Association for the Study of Negro Life, the National Urban League, the National Commission on Christian Education, the Association of American

Colleges, the General Conference of the Methodist Church, Hadassah (the Women's Zionist Organization of America), and the League of Women Voters. She also served on the boards of the Southern Conference Educational Fund, the American Council on African Education, the Council of Church Women, the Girl Scouts of Ameica, the Hyde Park Memorial for Franklin D. Roosevelt, and the National Committee on Atomic Information.

Bethune spent her last years at the Retreat, where the floor of her office was fashioned from the old boards of the original Faith Hall. A collection of autographed photographs lined the walls; tables and mantlepieces were used to exhibit her collection of elephant miniatures as well as many of the gifts she had received during her lifetime.

On May 17, 1954, Bethune became overjoyed at an announcement she had been hoping to hear for a long time: The Supreme Court ruled unanimously in the case of *Brown v. Board of Education of Topeka* that segregation in public schools was **unconstitutional**. Following this ruling, she wrote in her weekly column in the *Chicago Defender*:

The wise judges of the high bench saw, without difference of opinion among them at this point that America needs to provide for itself and for the Negro equality in fundamental education.

There can be no divided democracy, no class government, and no half-free country under the Constitution. Therefore, there can be no discrimination, no segregation, no separation of some citizens from the rights which belong to all citizens.

Bethune did not live long enough to see the *Brown* ruling take effect. She died of a heart attack at the age of 79 on May 18, 1955, and was buried on the campus of Bethune-Cookman College.

Since her death, Bethune has been awarded many posthumous honors. In 1973, she was inducted into the National Women's Hall of Fame. The following year, on what would have been her 99th birthday, a statue of Bethune made by sculptor Robert

An inspirational leader, Bethune continually urged young black women to achieve greatness. Without faith, nothing is possible," she said. "With it, nothing is impossible."

Berks was unveiled in Washington, D.C.'s Lincoln Park. The sculpture poignantly depicts Bethune leaning on her signature cane, handing a copy of her legacy to two young black children. In 1985, recognition continued when the U.S. Postal Service issued a commemorative stamp bearing her likeness.

Bethune often insisted that she had been blessed with a rich and wonderful life even though she had been born into poverty. She wrote in a magazine article entitled "My Last Will and Testament" that she wanted to pass on the richness of her life's experiences by inspiring acts of love and fellowship in others. Such a legacy, she hoped, would foster education and interracial cooperation. "Faith, courage, brotherhood, dignity, ambition, responsibility—these are needed today as never before," she wrote. "We must cultivate them and use them as tools for our task of completing the establishment of equality for the Negro."

An inspirational educator and an influential adviser to America's leaders, Mary McLeod Bethune worked tirelessly to make this dream of equality come true.

This U.S. postage stamp honors the legacy of Mary McLeod Bethune. It was issued in 1985 to commemorate the fiftieth anniversary of the founding of the National Council of Negro Women.

## RESEARCH PROJECT

In 1948, President Harry S. Truman ordered that the U.S. armed forces be desegregated so that black and white solders would serve together in combat units. Do some research on this decision. Why did Truman desegregate the armed forces? Why was this an important civil rights milestone for black Americans? Write a two-page paper.

## TEXT-DEPENDENT QUESTIONS

1. Why did many blacks assume that racial oppression would be eliminated in America after the United States entered World War II?
2. Why did Bethune resign as president of Bethune-Cookman College in 1942?
3. What was the "Declaration by Negro Voters" of 1944?

# RESOURCES

## FURTHER READING

Bell, Janet Dewart. *Lighting the Fires of Freedom: African American Women in the Civil Rights Movement*. San Francisco: The New Press, 2018.

Broadwater, Andrea. *Mary McLeod Bethune: Educator and Activist*. Berkeley Heights, N.J.: Enslow Publishers, 2003.

Jones, Ida E. *Mary McLeod Bethune in Washington, D.C.: Activism and Education in Logan Circle*. Charleston, S.C.: The History Press, 2013.

Robertson, Ashley N. *Mary McLeod Bethune in Florida: Bringing Social Justice to the Sunshine State*. Foreword by Dr. Gwendolyn Boyd. Charleston, S.C.: The History Press, 2015.

Schwartz, Heather E. *Mary McLeod Bethune: Education and Equality*. Huntington Beach, Calif.: Teacher Created Materials, 2017.

# INTERNET RESOURCES

**www.nps.gov/mamc/index.htm**
The National Park Service website for Mary McLeod Bethune tells about her life and the historic site of her Council House.

**http://myloc.gov/Exhibitions/naacp/Pages/Default.aspx**
The Library of Congress exhibition *The NAACP: A Century in the Fight for Freedom* provides information about the women and men who helped shape the organization during its first 100 years.

**www.pbs.org/wgbh/amex/eyesontheprize**
Based on the PBS American Experience television series *Eyes on the Prize: America's Civil Rights Movement 1954–1985*, this site links to profiles on people and documents from the time.

**www.aaregistry.org**
African American Registry is a comprehensive online storehouse of African American history and heritage. The website includes articles about African-American history and important people and moments in the Civil Rights Movement.

**www.splcenter.org**
The Southern Poverty Law Center (SPLC) monitors hate groups and other extremists throughout the U.S. and exposes their activities to law enforcement agencies, the media, and the public.

# INDEX

## ABOUT THE AUTHOR

Mary Hasday is an editor and writer. A graduate of Temple University in Philadelphia, she currently lives in London with her husband, Skylar Franks, and their three children.